INDIAN DIARY

Edward Ardizzone

INDIAN DIARY

1952–53

Introduction by
Malcolm Muggeridge

THE BODLEY HEAD

LONDON SYDNEY
TORONTO

British Library Cataloguing
in Publication Data
Ardizzone, Edward
Indian Diary
1. India — Description and travel —
Personal narratives
I. Title
915.4'04'4 DS 414
ISBN: 0–370–30525–6

© The Estate of Edward Ardizzone 1984
Printed in Great Britain for
The Bodley Head Ltd
9 Bow Street, London, WC2E 7AL
by Grosvenor Press
Set in Linotron Bembo Special
First published 1984

Contents

Publisher's note

In 1952 Edward Ardizzone was invited by UNESCO to take part in their Seminar for the Production of Audio-Visual Aids for Fundamental Education in India. He was a member of a four-man team that spent three months in Delhi and three in Bombay, from early November 1952 to the end of May 1953.

As was often his custom when away from home, Edward Ardizzone kept a daily diary of his stay, augmenting his written entries fully and freely by sketches in pencil and ink and, occasionally, in watercolour and pastel. When he returned to England Ardizzone began a series of Indian paintings (mostly watercolours) which were sold at a successful exhibition at The Leicester Galleries in London a year or so later. We have been able to trace only four of them.

No records of seminars of that time appear to have been kept by UNESCO so everything we know about this one must be deduced from Ardizzone's diary entries or his letters home. The Seminar team members were Ardizzone, Diva Bose, Abib Hussain and Norman McLaren. Norman McLaren is the well-known film maker and animator. Born in Scotland, he has lived in Canada and worked there for the National Film Board since 1941. His role at the Seminar was to teach the stu-

Extract from a letter to Philip Ardizzone (4½ × 7), 1952, (*pen*), Aingelda Ardizzone.
Reproduced by kind permission of the owner.

dents photography and how to make films, filmstrips and cartoons. Edward Ardizzone taught illustration and illustration reproduction, lithography and silk screen printing, the latter being something about which he admits, in a letter written at the time to his late son Philip, he was fairly ignorant. About the other members of the team we have been able to discover very little.

While he was in India Ardizzone kept closely in touch with England and he records in his diary commissions by *Vogue* and by *Punch*, the latter under the current editorship of Malcolm Muggeridge, who contributes the Introduction to this book. Norman McLaren, writing about Edward Ardizzone from his home in Montreal, regrets that 'time has effaced so many of the details of our Indian experience. I greatly admired his genius, his keen eye and swift spontaneous draughtsmanship. It always seemed a miracle to me how he could capture the character and atmosphere of people and places, often with amazing economy, out of a dash and swirl of lines, dots, squiggles, hatching and cross-hatching, the totality of which ended up in a delicately balanced and rounded-out composition . . . I do remember vividly and with affection what a most genial and delightful person Ardizzone was. He was a great companion. To work with him was a very real pleasure and experience. His cheerful spirit and unflappable nature were of immense value in guiding the activities, and overcoming the vicissitudes of that UNESCO project.'

Sketching

Getting into a Tonga

Trying to find the right shop

Illustrations from *Punch* 1 July 1953, (9 × 7½), signed Diz, ⟨pen⟩.
Reproduced by kind permission of *Punch*.

Introduction

I was particularly taken with Edward Ardizzone's *Indian Diary*; it is a fine example of his particular artistry in words and line that I came to appreciate as editor of *Punch*, and has for its subject the post-Raj Indian scene, to me particularly fascinating. I first became infatuated with India when, on going down from Cambridge in 1924, I went there to teach at an Indian Christian college at Alwaye in what was then Travancore, now Kerala. Then, ten years later, I joined the editorial staff of the *Calcutta Statesman* for a couple of years. Subsequently, I had various occasions for returning to India, one of the most interesting being to do the commentary for Kevin Billington's brilliant documentary *Twilight of Empire*, at roughly the same time as Ardizzone was in India doing his UNESCO stint.

When I became editor of *Punch* in January 1953, one of my first duties was to get to know the artists who contributed regularly to the magazine. They were, to me, a new and intriguing species; quite different from the writing variety who gathered noisily in El Vino's, and with whom I was all too familiar. In the artists I seemed to detect, underneath their smiles and sallies, a quiet melancholy. Purveyors of humour are, indeed, prone to sadness, which traditional clowns cover up by painting a huge white grin on their faces. Likewise, the great classics of humour mingle laughter and melancholy — witness, Chichikov in Gogol's *Dead Souls*, Cervantes's Knight of the Woeful Countenance in his *Don Quixote*, Falstaff in Shakespeare's *King Henry IV*, Mr Pooter in *The Diary of a Nobody* and P. G. Wodehouse's Jeeves and Bertie Wooster.

The artists in my time with *Punch* were a brilliant galaxy; I think, for instance, of Norman Mansbridge who produced, among many other good things, a splendid series of illustrations in colour of how the Pursuit of Happiness fantasy had worked out; of Leslie Illingworth, now, alas, dead, who contributed the weekly political cartoon with distinction; of the greatly talented Ronnie Searle, and so on. One of the artists, however, always seemed to me somehow different from the others, and I could only attribute this to his being more of an artist pure and simple than a fabricator or illustrator of jokes. This was Edward Ardizzone, whom I remember very vividly — large in bulk but gentle in manner; a distinguished art teacher as well as an outstanding practitioner.

It may be said that, in a sense, jokes are the curse of humour, as, for instance, violence is the curse of power and rhetoric the curse of oratory. Most humorous artists begin with a joke and work back to the humour, often losing it on the way. There was one famous *Punch* artist, George Belcher, who, following this procedure, so ran out of jokes that he had to be provided with one for his weekly contribution. Even then he ran into trouble; as, on one occasion, having been provided with a joke about a fishmonger's shop, he turned in a drawing of a greengrocer's shop, because, he explained, there was one near where he lived.

The joke, as such, plays little or no part in Ardizzone's drawings; he is more in the vein of a Charlie Chaplin than of a Bob Hope. It is the intrinsic absurdity of our human condition, the inexorable disparity between our aspirations and our achievements, that appeals to him rather than our particular absurdities. How I wish that, when I was editor of *Punch*, I had asked Ardizzone to illustrate the Fall of Man as a sort of celestial or cosmic version of the old banana-skin joke! He would have got the point, and done it beautifully.

One of the few things I took away with me when I left *Punch* was a print of one of Ardizzone's *Punch* covers in colour — this one for a special Autumn Number in the far-off days when the magazine's price was six-pence. Now I have it framed and hung in my study, and it gives me perpetual satisfaction. There is the tradition-al Mr Punch with his humpback, his cunning smile, and his little dog, Toby, wearing a ruff and standing up on his two legs. Autumn leaves are falling, and there is a besom leaning against a tree-trunk for sweeping them up. It is altogether a quite conventional ensemble, but notable because Mr Punch is not just a symbolic figure but in some mysterious way seems to be alive — a live-ly, mischievous, sharp-witted little man, curious about everyone and their ways, given to satire and ridicule, but never malignant — everything, in fact, that *Punch* magazine set out to be.

The illustrated diaries that Ardizzone produced all his

life are now collectors' items, and deservedly so. In them the words and the drawings match up perfectly together; one reads the pictures as naturally as one does the words. Ardizzone considered, and I think rightly, that the best of all his diaries was the one he kept in India, in 1952 and 1953, when he was there on a UNESCO mission concerned with audio-visual aids and silk-screen printing. Despite the coming of independence, the hand of the Raj was still heavily upon, particularly, the higher ranges of public education, with which the UNESCO project necessarily brought Ardizzone into contact.

It was a sort of twilight between an empire which had expired and an India and Pakistan which had lately come to pass. Ardizzone perfectly catches this scene as I remember it, in both his diary entries and drawings. Also, miraculously, he manages to sustain his equilibrium despite the tendency of his students to combine apparent eagerness to learn with indifference to the passage of time. With his all-embracing eye he takes in even mosquito-nets, and shows a would-be sleeper (himself in fact) struggling to adjust one (see page 114) — something I remember doing years and years ago.

Malcolm Muggeridge

INDIAN DIARY

The Diary

3rd November 1952, Monday
Arrive Orly, cloud and rain, four hr. wait. Leave 2.00.
First stop Geneva. Fly at 20,000 and arrive between a
rainbow. First snow on the hills. Have rearmost seat.
Priest and very old woman put in front. Excellent late
lunch. Brilliant sunshine with blanket of cloud below.

Geneva — Milan — above a tremendous cloud layer,
bit of evening sun. Snow-covered Alps glimpsed in
gaps between the clouds directly below us. Milan at
dusk. Dark when we start for Rome. Curious way of
travelling. No chance to make friends with fellow pas-
sengers.

Rome — Athens — Cairo. Leave Cairo at dawn.
Catholic priest going to Nepal. Brandy and coffee at
Athens airport. Looked pretty at night. Somehow less
efficient and stereotyped than others. Stay in plane in
Cairo. Hope to sleep. Army of cleaners. No good.

4th November 1952, Tuesday
Desert, Red Sea and desert. Basra. Palms and mud
along Euphrates. Airport pretty dingy but has more
character than most. Only short stay there. Getting very
hot but dry and not unpleasant. The mouth of the
Euphrates. Mud and blue. Like a butterfly's wing but
horrid.

5th November 1952, Wednesday

Arrive Delhi Airport at dawn after two days' flying. By car to Maiden's Hotel. The approach to Delhi looked enchanting in the half-light. Many peasants on the road, a string of camels, booths being opened up beside the road, a great castle with minarets and fine trees. Feel that dawn is the right time to approach a city for the first time. One's first impression is of its waking up. The hotel pretentious, the breakfast execrable and my room pretty poor for £2 a day. Meet Attegalle on his way to Mysore. The project seems to be taking on formidable proportions. Take a taxi to Min. of E and keep it waiting. Meet Dr Shukla and Humayun Kabir and both clever and nice. Back for lunch. Very hot curry and very large lager. Sleep after lunch and wake at dusk. Kites and pigeons in the trees outside my door, also very active grey squirrels. Whisky at 7/6 a double and a large bottle of beer about the same. Will have to give up drinking.

6th November 1952, Thursday

See Dr Pires at Central Institute of Education. Am toured the establishment and see the venue of our Seminar. Submissive little art master. I can see all sorts of difficulties. Pires charming but with him Chief Education Officer of a province — real schoolmaster. Didn't like him and as I had not a doctorate he didn't like me. The building very new and partly unfinished and dedicated to training teachers and research in teaching. Had that rather unpleasant, bright, earnest quality of all small provincial universities. Classes on psychology, child welfare and the crafts. Taxi to Imperial Bank, New

Wed Nov. 5th 1952

Arrive Delhi Airport at dawn after 2 days flying. By car to Maidens Hotel. The approach to Delhi looked enchanting in the ½ light. Many peasants on the road a string of camels, booths being opened up beside the road, a great castle with minarets and fine trees. Feel that dawn is the right time to approach a city for the 1st time, one's first impression is of it waking up. The Hotel pretentious. The breakfast execrable & my room pretty poor for £2 a day. — Meet Altzgalle on his way to Mysore — The project seems to be taking on formidable proportions —

Thursday 6ᵗʰ

See Dr Prin at Central institute of
Education — Am loaned the establishment
& see the Venue of our Seminar —
Submission little art Master. I can see
all sorts of difficulties — Prins charming
but with him chief Education officer of a
province — real schoolmaster didn't like
him, & as I had not a doctorate he didn't
like me. . The building very new &
partly unfinished & dedicated to training
teachers & research in teaching — Heard
that rather unpleasant bright earnest
quality of all small provincial universities
classes on physycology. Child Welfare & the crafts

Taxi to imperial
bank. New Delhi
find to have come
to it wrong branch.
lunch at the
imperial —
large & flash.

Tea with
Doris.

Dinner at

the maidens Hotel & work in my
room.

Delhi. Find I have come to wrong branch. Lunch at the Imperial. Large and flash. Tea with Doris[1]. Dinner at Maiden's Hotel and work in my room.

7th November 1952, Friday

Taxi to Imperial Bank, Delhi, and after fearful struggle get my money. The bank a seeming pandemonium in which one wanders from desk to desk behind the grille, with papers piled high on desks and floors and countless clerks. Then a tremendous rush to Jamia Milia and see Hamid Ali Khan and staff of the Jamia publishing house. Found them quiet and charming and very humble but no need to be. I fear I talked too much and some nonsense to boot. Called in on Doris and refunded loan. Back at Maiden's Hotel for late lunch. Taxi 16 rupees.

In evening walk through Nicholson Gardens and through a gate in a fortified wall into the old city. A fascinating glimpse of a crowded native street. The gardens fine with many great trees. Hordes of children playing football or cricket. Greener than I expected but very dusty, a dust which turned the evening light into a gold fog.

The complexity of costumes and life generally makes it impossible for me to draw yet. Must get some drawings of details from life first.

8th November 1952, Saturday

Walk in some nearby gardens and try and have a look at the Jumna[2] River but see mostly gravel beds.

To Imperial Hotel for lunch with Doris. What strikes me so much about Delhi and suburbs is the combination of extreme newness and age, nothing in between. New universities, institutes, government buildings, schools,

After lunch walk from Cannaught
Place to Secretariat
+ spend 2 hours making

hats & drawings — Much of
the time on a bench in the park

flats, etc. After lunch walk from Connaught Place to Secretariat and spend two hours making notes and drawings. Much of the time on a bench in the park in front of the Secretariat. To tea with Humayun Kabir. Officials from the ministry and their wives congregated in the garden. The Secretary for Education guest of honour. Very interesting on the subject of Russia which he had just visited. I found making conversation with the ladies somewhat difficult, though one, a pretty girl, was very chatty. Find that they really don't know English very well.

Walk some way home with a minor official. Very talkative and a great bore. Back to Maiden's Hotel for dinner. The city extremely dusty and the effect of golden haze in the evening due to this. I shall be longing for some rain soon, though I gather there will be none.

9th November 1952, *Sunday*
Find a church just across the way so to Mass at 8.00. A cosmopolitan crowd of Europeans, taking the front seats. Some had the air of coming from embassies. I take a back seat and find myself behind Dr Pires and family.

I spend the day lazily in my room reading, going over my notes and trying out some plastic. Go for a walk in the evening.

10th November 1952, *Monday*
In my room all day drawing and writing. Usual evening walk, through Nicholson Gardens into Old Delhi and back another route. Road in the shadow of the city wall and shaded too by big trees. Girls getting into a pony *gharri* making a wonderful colour note in the dusky evening light. Deep violet blue, orange, crimson &

(25)

of golden haze in the evening
due to this. I shall be longing
for some rain soon, though I
gather there will be none.

white. *Gharri* burnt sienna, earth pinkish, grey green leaves and pink glow from sunset. The old town a splendid but squalid confusion of stalls, booths, shops and a milling crowd of pedestrians and cyclists.

Dinner with Karl Borch at the Servis Hotel. Other guest a Pole called Rutgaber. A pleasant evening and I drink a lot of whisky.

11th November 1952, Tuesday

To Central Inst. of Ed. in morning and discuss materials for class. In the evening walk along the road by the Jumna as far as the railway bridge and back. The road for some way skirted the city wall, above the battlements on which could be seen a romantic huddle of houses. The road was lined with many trees under which was a conglomeration of mud, basket work and tin huts inhabited by whole families. Here too were many sacred cows and some bulls lying penned in or roaming freely. A herd of goats and their kids passed by. The trees, in spite of the crowds of people, were thickly populated with hooded crows, little striped squirrels and great kites, and flocks of small birds. At one place under the wall, which was quite 40ft high, was a timber yard where men naked to the waist were sawing big logs by hand. After following the wall for about half a mile, I took a left turn towards the banks of the river. Here seemed to be a sort of sacred ground. There were huts which housed shrines. The dark interiors looked neat and clean and seem to sparkle with tinsel decorations. In one an old man was intoning from a book. Then there was a little yellow stucco temple in which a woman was kneeling at the altar dimly seen.

(27)

Sunday 9th Nov.

Find a church just across the way
so to Mass at 8·00.

A cosmopolitan crowd of Europeans —
taking the front seats — Come here to air
of coming from Embassies. — I take
a back seat and find myself behind
Dr. Paies & family

I spend the day lazifying in my room
reading, going over my notes &
trying out some plastic

Go for a walk in the Evening.

<u>Monday 10th.</u>

From here the road turned right to follow the river bank and between it and the river was a line of huts and mini-ature mosque-like structures shaded by low trees and all screened from the road by basket-work fences. Through the gateways, which had written signs on them, one glimpsed a figure sitting on a low bed in meditation or women sweeping an already tidy ground. Occasionally one saw the river which ran under a steep bank, with here and there steps leading down to it.

In the street, threading their way between the bullock carts, cows, horses and cyclists, were a few fearful-looking men with wild matted hair and staring eyes. They were stark naked except for a minute codpiece and were covered in dust and ochre.

On the way back saw a bevy of women dressed in splendid colours, saffron and tomato red, orange, green, pale lilac. They glowed like jewels. Walked back through a little park in the short twilight. Very calm and peaceful. Sit and write and draw until 7.00 when McLaren turns up.

12th November 1952, Wednesday
A leisurely morning pottering, making notes and talk-ing to McLaren. In the afternoon to the Secretariat and abortive conference. Diva Bose with us but the fourth member, Hussain, not there. Nothing much decided. Back to the hotel with Bose to have tea. Attegalle turns up. Hear the good news that the Indian Government pays our hotel bills. Dine with McLaren and Attegalle and get much business, especially financial, tidied up. No time to make a drawing.

Very late lunch at the
Imperial then call on the
M.P. for Mysore at the
~~Parliament~~ House —
Building much more —
impressive inside than
out — Walk round
the 1st floor colonnade
with the M.P. & then
have tea in a stately
room.

Visit a new Bhuddist
temple on way home at
the hour of evening prayer — Great
noise of clashing [cymbals] & drums —
Men & women standing & praying before
various
altars or shrines ? ? ?
in which great
statues —

Musicians
playing in another
hall — Women
& children sitting
on the floor —
The man
spinning round
& round
something
unpleasing
about
everything.

Obviously a show place with tourists
welcome.

13th November 1952, Thursday

Exhausting conference at Ministry, Shah, Abib
Hussain, Diva Bose, Attegalle, McLaren and myself.
Main item, the themes to be employed, not decided.
Very late lunch at the Imperial and then call on the MP
for Mysore at the Parliament House. Building much
more impressive inside than out. Walk round the first-
floor colonnade with the MP and then have tea in a
stately room.

Visit a new Buddhist temple on way home at the hour
of evening prayer. Great noise of clashing cymbals and
drums. Men and women standing praying before
various altars and shrines in which great statues. Musicians playing in another hall. Women and children sitting on the floor. The man spinning round and round.
Something unpleasant about everything. Obviously a
showplace with tourists welcome.

In the evening dine with Attegalle at a real Indian restaurant. Good partridge, curry and many side dishes.

14th November 1952, Friday

To Ministry at 10.00 and confer till 12.30, Abib Hussain, Attegalle, McLaren and I. More decisions this
time. After various calls and late lunch at the Imperial
we then went some eleven miles out of Delhi to Ajanta
College, a tiny village crafts school situated in what
looked like converted farm buildings. Principal away so
didn't stay long. The country flat and very dusty. From
the glimpses we had of them, the villages looked very
pretty, a huddle of brick and one or two stucco buildings among trees. Back to Maiden's in time for a quick
tea and crash and then to some Indian friends of Atte-

round in a bare room & talked — pastry
confections & tea served — Talked much —
with Biswas a painter & of whose conversation
I only understood 1 word in 4,
As I was most anxious to get on with him
in the hope of help for the class this was
very exhausting. — So much I drew here

galle where we spent the evening. We sat round in a
bare room and talked. Pastry confections and tea served.
Talked much with Biswas, a printer, of whose conversation I only understood one word in four. As I was
most anxious to get on with him in the hope of help for
the class this was very exhausting. So much to draw
here and no chance or time to draw it yet. A very tiring
day, so much uncertainty as to printing materials, cash
from the Ministry, etc.

15th November 1952, *Saturday*

To Jamia Milia in the morning to attend a Festival. The
river quadrangle decked with booths, a bandstand in the
centre with boys playing bagpipes. Speeches under a
great canvas awning. Children reciting poetry. Am
taken round to see the exhibits, children's paintings,
charts and specimens of Adult Education. Order myself
a pair of slippers. Back to New Delhi, lunch at the
Imperial, say goodbye to Attegalle, shop and return to
hotel. Way to Jamia Milia goes past many tombs,
among which set some distance from the road is
Humayun's[3]. Walk with McLaren in evening. To
Jumna again but streets very empty and no naked holy
men. Back by way of the old city. Crowded streets.
Buy fruit at stall. Back just before dark. Pass on our
route many black and white oxen, some standing being
milked, and others drawing carts. Also a great huddle
of refugee encampments.

16th November 1952, *Sunday*

Kept waiting all day by Biswas, the horror, but found
him very useful when he did arrive. The real vulgarian
but with careful handling may be more useful still.

To Doris and Bill[4] in the evening and with them see a show of indifferent sculpture, arty and affected. Then to Moti Mahal where we eat roast chicken in our fingers sitting in their roof restaurant. Back at 10.00.

17th November 1952, Monday

Morning at the Central Institute with regard to accommodation and supplies. Talked to Shukla on the phone to find that he is backing down on the question of supplies. It looks as if there will be another battle. Maddening, as all arrangements were completed and agreed to by Attegalle.

To *The Times of India* press where I have arranged for typescript to be printed in double quick time. First satisfactory, cut and dried bit of business. Let's hope it turns out as such.

18th November 1952, Tuesday

To the Chawri Bazaar with Norman and Jeswami to choose paper. An extraordinary higgledy piggledy of small open shops, arcades and stalls in a narrow street. Have great difficulty in finding our shop which turns out to be no shop at all but the business premises of a big paper dealer. We have a most successful interview with the manager and bespeak some excellent but cheap paper.

From there to Dhormural in Connaught Place. Lunch at the Imperial. Have a five-minute interview with Shukla which extends to one and a half hours. Home at about five.

19th November 1952, Wednesday

Ministry car doesn't turn up. To Biswas by taxi. Meet Elvin there from HMSO. Biswas, with printer and

us a view of his works. — Hoover
not bad printed work considering limited
material. All much excited about
plastic material — Nice young artists
employed — not very good but can learn
to improve — One had bought a copy
of Tony's Foray [?] Soya [?] for sake of
drawing. Hope B. will supply our
chemicals for litho. Drive back
to Maroni [?] for lunch.

Had £11 worth of rupees taken from
my pocket — a sad blow.

artists in tow, takes us a tour of his works. Not bad printed work considering limited material. All much excited about plastic material. Nice young artists employed, not very good but anxious to improve. One had brought a copy of Tony's *Forsyte Saga*[5] for sake of drawings. Hope B will supply our chemicals for litho. Driven back to Maiden's for lunch.

Back to New Delhi in afternoon. Buy drawing board, squeegee, rollers, rum and fresh limes. Wait for McL at the Coffee House. Get back 6.30.

20th November 1952, *Thursday*

To Imperial Bank when we notice some splendid painted backcloths for street photographers. Then to India House photolitho press to find Biswas and lunch at the Imperial. After lunch call on Sen at *The Hindustan Standard* where we are shown round the press.

From there to the Chawri Bazaar where we leave the car by the mosque and walk the streets in search of brushes and paints. See a Hindu wedding procession. The bridegroom garlanded and riding a horse. Banner bearers behind him and ahead drummers, pipe players, dancers carrying striped batons which they clashed together, and a Sikh bagpipe band. The noise tremendous. The balconies of the houses lined with people and the street crowded. The bridegroom, a good-looking boy in a turban, looked rather sheepish. Had £15 worth of ruppees taken from my pocket — a sad blow.

21st November 1952, Friday
In the morning by taxi to Old Delhi. Sit in taxi and
make drawings of the photographers' pitches. Some
splendid material here but so complicated. Colour
note — dark heads of young men, blue black hair,
warm black skins, blue shirts, bent together and against
the gradated cold blue of the backcloth. Also visible,
ochre, Indian red and green of painted buildings and
trees in backcloth. All dark in key. Beside photographers a pretty glimpse through windows into the
primary school. Rows of little children squatting on the
floor. Dark but much reflected light. The usual crowd
of beggars. White cattle. Country women. The oppo-
site side of the road a huddle of booths, huts, motor-
cycles, *gharris*, under feathery trees. The diffusion of light
makes it very difficult to grasp form. The Rowlandson
approach, a linear one, would seem the best. Move to
the Chawri Bazaar and draw the buildings on one side of
the street. Taxi parked by many ox carts, with oxen
lying and resting. Moslem women like white pyramids
topped by little white crowns. A party of countrymen
outside a clothing stall. They carried bundles and staffs.

Visit a jeweller and look at his collection of antique
jewellery. The nicest pieces about 700 rupees. Far too
expensive for me. Back to Maiden's for lunch.

22nd November 1952, Saturday
To Probyn Road and meet the bulk of our trainees. I
chat with the artists and see some of their work, particularly one from the District Education Officer who is
producing a nicely designed and illustrated paper and
who has knowledge of printing methods, etc. Large

Sat: 22 — to Probyn Road
& meet the bulk of our trainees
& chat with the artists & see
some of their work — Particularly of
one from the District Education officer —
who is producing a nicely designed &
illustrated paper & who has knowledge
of printing methods etc — Large work
in paint very bad — but illustration
not bad at all.

work in paint very bad, but illustrations not bad at all.

Afternoon spent in drawing and writing in my room.

In the evening go to Maktaba Jamia where we dine with Jamia Milia and a young professor. Proper Indian food which was deliciously varied in flavour. Curds with a mutton pilau, fried meat balls. Then meat with a brown curry sauce and a sweet to follow. The sweet a sort of stiff, white milk-shape affair with a little bit of fine silver paper which is eaten as well.

23rd November 1952, Sunday

Work all day in my room, chiefly writing letters. The young Indian from *The Times of India* came to tea with me. At 5.00 take taxi to Parliament Street to see the Children's Art Show but fail to find it and come home.

24th November 1952, Monday

Our first day at the Seminar and an exhausting one. A bit of a muddle to start with, with trainees getting bored towards end of morning. Hints of didactic scepticism from the Bihar party, with the sprightly dark chap in the lead. Feel that the workers in Social Education think they know more about the problems than their teachers, which is probably true. Things brighten up after Norman's showing of film strips in the afternoon — lucky man. He has a new skill and technique to teach — most attractive to artists. Some bright practical artists among the bunch but none with an 'A'. Towards end of day students arriving without accommodation to go to. Norman doing good work on the phone with Shukla. Full marks to him. To dinner with Elvin.

25th November 1952, Tuesday

Another exhausting day at the School. Things getting

Afternoon spent in drawing +
writing in my room.

In the evening go to Makhtaba Jamia
where we dine with Hamid Ali Khan,
the Director of Jamia Milia + a young
professor.

Proper Indian
food which was
deliciously varied
in flavour —
Curds with
a mutton pilau.
Fried meat balls.
Then meat with a
brown curry sauce + a sweet to follow.
The sweet a sort of stiff white
milk shape affair with a little bit of
fine silver paper which we eat as well.

'Countrymen in the Bazaar – Delhi' (6½ × 8¾), signed EA, 1952, (*pen and watercolour*), The Arts Council of Great Britain. Reproduced by kind permission of the owners.

into shape a little. Nothing to draw.

26th November 1952, *Wednesday*

A day much as before. Lecture for one and a half hours
in the afternoon on the processes of reproduction, of
which a third understand very little, the three stupidest
trainees being two art teachers and our one lady pupil
who hasn't a clue about anything. Shall leave Norman
to take her in hand. The dark gentleman from Bihar and
his group as sceptical as ever. A number of trainees so
concerned about the cost of their quarters that they can't
think of anything else. Fear the class may dissolve into a
riot. One bright spot. A few intelligent young men who
are very interested in Norman's film strip technique.
After class have tea with head of Delhi Public Library
who argues most ably for about two hours that the
whole policy of Adult Education here is mistake. Come
away with one's brain in a whirl and only recover after a
very big tot of rum.

27th November 1952, *Thursday*

An easier day at the class. Norman gives an interesting
talk on animated cartoons which gives me a chance to
draw some of the students.

   To dinner with a Mr and Mrs Caughley, a NZ
psychologist, at the Swiss Hotel. Turns out to be a large
party. Meet Dr Philips of the British Council and other
pleasant people.

28th November 1952, *Friday*

Class as usual. See a performance on the stage of playlets
and dancing by children. Some of the simple dancing
very pretty. Continue my talk on processes of reproduction. Get bogged down on photogravure. Talk with

(48)

To drive into a Mr. & Mrs.
Caughley, a N.Z. physchologist
~~first~~ at the Lewis Hotel.
Turns out to be a large
party. Met Dr.
Philips of the British
Council & other
pleasant people.

the dark gentleman of Bihar and think he might co-operate. Shukla calls in towards end of class. I get my hair cut.

29th November 1952, Saturday
Seminar in the morning. To a party at the Cecil in the afternoon. Party given by Leilgeher, a sort of farewell one to see his pictures. Great crowd there of various notables from British Council, UNESCO and the embassies. Am introduced to the Papal nuncio, a Monsignor who claims me as a brother Piedmontese.

A Child's description of God.
God by Jyoti Sahi, 6 years old
God is the wind. He goes to countrees and countrees with big puffs like wolves breth. God is the sun and shines with big strayt bits like swords sparkling out. And the leeves rustle with the wind while the little little birds fly in the sky. And all the trees bend down like a dell when the wind rustles in them. And the sun flowers look up at the sun beautifooly like other suns looking at the grayt sun. God looks at the roses and says 'Look at the sun and you will get strong.'

30th November 1952, Sunday
Doris to lunch, with Mr and Mrs Caughley to drinks before. Sit on the lawn in front of the hotel and chat. Work for some time in my room, then stroll in the evening to find a pretty bit of landscape.

are as a body piecemeal.

1st December 1952, Monday

Quiet day at the school, it being a Muslim holiday and only a few students in attendance. Sketch out a strip cartoon in evening to show the class that a story can be told without words.

2nd December 1952, Tuesday

Take the dim schoolmaster with me shopping supplies for the class. A long session buying brushes, powder colours and other materials. In the afternoon Norman gives his talk on the core of experience. Afterwards an inconclusive discussion on the subject of our next topic to be illustrated.

As well as shopping, visit the bank and cash a cheque for £50. Paying hotel bill in the evening.

3rd December 1952, Wednesday

Feel that we are makng some progress in the Seminar. The D[ark] G[entleman] from B[ihar] (Shrivastava) gives a highly dramatic talk on the power of drama as an Education in Fundamentals. Another very tiring day. Bose complains that it will be difficult for him to live on a vegetarian diet in the south. What about N and I from the West! We don't complain. The man's a fusspot. I wish that neither he nor Mr Hussain were accompanying us.

4th December 1952, Thursday

A hectic day. Huss turns out trumps in getting accommodation for outside students here. Meet big white chief of C[entral] I[nstitute] Ed. Shown new classrooms which we are to inhabit. At last some sort of division among the trainees and a programme fixed. In the afternoon I talk on Book Production which was so well

(53)

understood, or seemed to be, that I galloped through it in under an hour. The DG from B suggested that I should continue on the subject of Proof Readers' Symbols which flummoxed me, however I think I managed to get out of it gracefully, without the loss of too much face.

5th December 1952, Friday

Move to Constitution House in the evening. A vast area of parallel one-storey buildings connected by an immense corridor. Each line of buildings arcaded on one side. Alone in my room I try the bathroom to find it occupied by a female of indeterminate age washing her hair. Some consternation on both sides and I beat a hasty retreat. Learn later that we have to share the bathroom. As it contains a shower and lavatory, all inadequately screened, our washing times will have to be fixed.

The inhabitants a curiously mixed lot. In my block a number of Indian families complete with children, a family to a large room, the lady with whom I have to share a bathroom next door, as well as others who I have not been able to determine. Everybody seems to camp out in the arcade which is littered with beds, chairs and bric-à-brac. By my door is a rabbit hutch containing a white rabbit. My room, which is like all the others, large, lofty with a raftered ceiling, a few pieces of rather cheap furniture painted brown, and a very hard bed. Cold during the night, plus a very hard pillow, made sleep difficult.

complete with children . a family
to , large , room . The lady with
whom I leave & clean a bathroom
next door, as well as others
who I have not been able to
determine . Everybody seems
to camp out in the arcade
which is littered with beds
chairs & bric a brac — by
my door is a rabbit hutch
containing a white rabbit .
My room which is like all
the others, large lofty with
a raftered ceiling , a few
pieces of rather cheap furniture
painted brown & a very hard
bed . — Cold during the night plus a very hard
pillow made sleep difficult .
Saturday 6 . Stayed late at the Institute
arranging the new furniture for our new class
rooms — A late lunch at a Chinese restaurant
with Norman .

Saturday 7th. Cold during night — Wake very
early wanting to p. to find the lady next
door usually ensconced in it lavatory — & there
for ages — Will have to get a pot. My boy
then brings me tea at 6.20 instead of 7.30
so altogether a disturbed morning —
to Mass at it Cathedral — 8.20. — painting of the
~~last supper~~ behind it main
altar one of it
worst I have seen.

In it afternoon
I tea with
Boris & Bill
who tell me
to my

consternation that I share my wash place
with a crazy Hungarian of doubtful morals &
a bad painter
to boot. Just
my luck.

6th December 1952, Saturday
Stayed late at the Institute arranging the new furniture
for our new classrooms. A late lunch at a Chinese restaurant with Norman.

Return to Friday. Norman and I find ourselves seated
at dinner with a large gentleman wearing a silk embroidered scarf. He was a member of the Upper House. We
learned that CH inhabited primarily by MPs and their
families but there were other people of all nationalities,
including sixty Buchmanites over here on a Moral
Rearmament drive. I noticed both Japs and Chinese
among the diners. Back to Saturday.

N and I go shopping later. I buy a pillow, nail scissors
and get a prescription made up. N buys blankets and
other things. Meet by chance some friends of his and
have coffee. Back for dinner at Constitution House.
Meet our large gentleman from the Upper House again.

7th December 1952, Sunday
Cold during night. Wake very early wanting to pee, to
find the lady next door well ensconced in the lavatory — and there for ages. Will have to get a pot. My
boy then brings me tea at 6.20 instead of 7.30, so
altogether a disturbed morning.

To Mass at the cathedral, 8.20. Painting of The Last
Supper behind the main altar one of the worst I have
seen. In the afternoon to tea with Doris and Bill who tell
me to my consternation that I share my washplace with
a crazy Hungarian of doubtful morals, a bad painter to
boot. Just my luck.

In the evening Norman and I go to dinner with
J[eswami]. What we thought would be a hideously dull

evening, turned out to be a delightful one. J's house, or rather shack, in a new suburb of mean shops and other shacks like J's. We dined seven strong in a tiny room. There were three guests, two art teachers and a lady English teacher besides Norman and myself, then J and his very pretty daughter. Mrs J did not dine with us but sat among her cooking pots in the kitchen. The dinner excellent but felt guilty eating it as I am sure J could not afford it. Before dinner we were introduced to two of the younger children, a little girl of eleven and a five-year-old boy, both pretty pets. Everybody very much in their Sunday best.

Home by bus and then by tonga. Our driver a merry fellow who whipped up his rather jaded horse to a gallop and continually jangled a peal of rather pretty bells. What one remembers best of the dinner — how pretty the lady teacher and J's daughter looked framed against the dark of the open doorway, the sound of rhythmic religious music coming from some far-off shacks, J's pictures NBG, oil lamps, the small half-covered courtyard and the fact that in cold weather the family of seven have to crowd into two minute rooms and one even smaller kitchen.

8th December 1952, *Monday*

Another very arduous day at the Institute. We move into our new quarters so not much work done. Visited by an elderly art teacher with grizzled hair and a grey stubble on his chin. I was tired and he was so sad that he almost moved me to tears. He had never been taught to draw life but only geometrical drawings, patterns and mechanical drawings. His method of teaching his pupils

wealth [?] the family of seven have to crowd
into 2 minute rooms & one even smaller
kitchen.

Monday 8 — Another very arduous day at
the institute — we move into our new
quarters so not much work done

Visited by an
elderly art teacher
with grizzled hair
& a grey stubble on
his chin. I was
tired & he was so
sad that he almost
moved me to tears.
He had never been
taught to draw life,
had only geometrical
drawings, patterns
& mechanical drawings.
His method of teaching
his pupils was to place
a teapot or some object on a table, make a
diagram drawing of it on the black-board &
instruct his pupils to copy his drawing.
He had arrived at the idea that
I had some magic trick
to impart which would
enable him to draw
figures, and the hope
that I would enrol
him in the seminar.
Of course I could not
enrol him & it was
his pathetic resignation that made me
almost weep — Resignation to teaching little
boys geometrical drawings but he was so glad
to work & doing it on starvation wages —

was to place a teapot or some object on a table, make a diagram drawing of it on the blackboard and instruct his pupils to copy his drawing. He had arrived with the idea that I had some magic trick to impart which would enable him to draw figures and with the hope that I would enrol him in the Seminar. Of course I could not enrol him and it was his pathetic resignation that made me almost weep. Resignation to teaching little boys geometrical drawings till he was too old to work and doing it on starvation wages. In fact the art masters here are hopeless. We have too many of them in the class as it is.

Taken to see a show of pictures by children at a neighbouring school. As usual the children's work, in spite of material disadvantages, showed signs of real beauty and vividness. The teachers' work execrable beyond belief. Feel mine is too but I am too tired to draw.

9th December 1952, *Tuesday*

Settled into our new rooms at CIE and more work been done by the class. Visitors to my room before dinner, a Canadian and American printer. Away goes the rest of my rum. Then the head of Jamia Milia and Dr Abib Hussain. They really want me to do a design for them.

10th December 1952, *Wednesday*

Kedar Nath, I and Jeswami all labour to produce a poster in stencil, three-quarter down, but not very good. Stupidity of KN makes difficulties. However he is a willing ox, but teaching him is like teaching a baby. Return tired with a bad leg and have to write an appreciation of the boys' school Art Show and think of designs for Jamia Milia.

Boot Nath's & Dua's Stencil posters look
promising — both of Raina & Massey doing
their vulgar little scribbles, but actually
making a show at last with paste up
of type..   Galvija's work looks well
designed —   Feel at last that my
section i beginning to show results &
creating more interest — So far it has
been the Cinderella to the photographer's
prince charming —

The dining room laid for a great banquet for the Moral Rearmament group. Waited as long as one could in the hope to see it.

11th December 1952, Thursday

This is like teaching little children. One has almost to show them how to put in drawing pins. However, by dint of unremitting personal attention and drawing over the artists' work oneself, some improved results are beginning to show.

Both Nath's and Dua's stencil posters look promising. Raina and Massey doing their vulgar little scribbles but actually making a show at last with paste-up of type. Galviya's work looks well designed. Feel at last that my section is beginning to show results and creating more interest. So far it has been the Cinderella to the photographer's Prince Charming.

12th December 1952, Friday

Money crisis becomes acute. Norman and I transported in turn on the back of Kirmani motor bike to the UNESCO Seminar office where we manage to borrow between us 100 rupees. However, N receives cable to say that money is on its way so all should be well soon.

Take Madiah Gowda out to dinner. Leave choice of restaurant to him. Alas, he would not believe that we liked Indian food so took us to a semi-Westernised restaurant. However, he promised to give us a real Madrasy dinner tomorrow night. Gowda a quiet elderly man with not much to say. A sombre lot, these Indians.

Getting much colder and Constitution House tenanted by forms wrapped in blankets.

13th December 1952, *Saturday*
With Kirmani to the bazaar to buy silk, paints and glue,
etc. for the silk screen process. Usual difficulty to find
anything one wanted. Find I get exhausted by the end-
less argument entailed in shopping, as well as the
crowded streets and extraordinary complexity of the
scene. I got bad tempered in consequence and inclined
to shout.

Madiah Gowda gives us our promised dinner at the
Madras Hotel. Delicious — rice and *chippatis* (very
light) served on large electroplated tray, one for each of
us. Then side dishes of vegetables, chutneys and curry
sauce, with more cool and hot buttery sauces in glasses.
The technique was to add in turn the sauces to one's
rice, plus spoonfuls of ghee added by the waiter, then
knead all together well with the fingers of the right hand
and eat. More difficult than it sounds. At the end, curds
poured over the remains of one's rice and a glass of
buttermilk to drink.

14th December 1952, *Sunday*
To Mass early with Doris and Bill, then a South Indian
breakfast with Norman and Madiah Gowda at a cafe —
round, white buns of a bread-like texture, curry sauce,
ground spices, pancakes containing very hot curried
vegetables. Coffee.

Engage our boy in the afternoon — Samuel
Thomas — has glowing references but feel he may be
stupid.

15th December 1952, *Monday*
An exasperating morning. Send out for nails and the
wrong size brought back. Only half the paints arrive

(65)

and the wrong lacquer. Don't stretch the silk enough and have to re-do. A continual stream of the wrong advice from the trainees. Lose my temper and inveigh against the country and in fact make an ass of myself.

To the Caughleys at 7.30. Farewell party to Borch. Home at midnight with no dinner but snacks.

16*th December* 1952, *Tuesday*

Feel ill, the result of whisky and no dinner. Quiet day at the Seminar. See Biswas in evening. My fire lighted by Samuel Thomas. Very pleasant and cosy.

17*th December* 1952, *Wednesday*

Another quiet day at the Seminar. Money shortage again acute as cabled money not arrived. N and I take Hussain, Bose and Gowda out to dinner. Very sticky evening to begin with. Gowda didn't like Bose or the Chinese food. The restaurant empty and rather dismal. Food not too good. However some useful clarification of the situation with regard to Mysore.

18*th December* 1952, *Thursday*

To Doris and Bill after dinner. Walk back.

Much of the day at the Seminar spent in making the small silk screen press in slow stages while being photographed by the camera boys to make an instructional strip film.

19*th December* 1952, *Friday*

Norman gets his money. Hope mine comes soon. Hussain takes us to dinner at the house of a Colonel Zaidi, a rich MP. The dinner lives up to the palatial quality of his bungalow and car. A 'Biriyani' — special *pilau* full of nuts (almonds and pistachios), chicken, a very long grained rice and sultanas. A side dish of yoghourt and

cucumber. Quite delicious. Bose and Gowda and a
bearded parliamentarian, older than other guests. The
talk at first political and then on art, literature, etc. Very
much in the manner of dining tables of the West. This
was the old world and one felt at home in it. Before
leaving the Seminar had to attend the start of the CIE
Foundation Day celebrations. Some interminable
speeches and then a pageant of Indian folklore. Glad to
get away early.

20th December 1952, Saturday
Wake up feeling very tired and depressed. My cash
arrives. Open an account at Lloyds and cash a cheque.
Stay on at the Institute in afternoon to try out a drawing
on the silk screen. All sorts of problems occurring.
Wonder if get any result at all? Asked to attend a party
of Indian journalists before dinner. Much whisky.
Found the journalists just like Western ones. The same
shop. They all drank whisky and all gave me the hor-
rors, with talk of corruption in high quarters and to a
man left wing or distinctly pinkish.

21st December 1952, Sunday
To the CIE at noon and stay there till five trying, with
the aid of Jeswami, to produce a silk screen print. Alas,
something goes badly wrong. The wrong materials —
and, after unavailing efforts to wash the tusche out,
have to destroy the screen and make a new one.

Sit up late writing.

22nd December 1952, Monday
A day with signs of possible progress. Try corn starch
with litho ink on a trial piece of silk. Seems to work.
Squeegees being made. Two new students (artists). One

dismal young chap and a saucy young woman. Very
tired at end of day, with a bad leg. Litho plates arrive.

23rd December 1952, *Tuesday*
Very tired and my leg hurts. I fear my drawings show
it.

24th December 1952, *Wednesday*
Take day off. Shopping in the morning. Afternoon and
evening spent in reading and writing. Feel much rested.

Christmas Day 1952
Mass early. To Norman's room where we received a
deputation from Jeswami and four of the photographers. They brought us gifts of a bunch of flowers
each, a box of halva and a Kashmiri carving each which
was most touching.

To lunch with Doris and Bill. A large party. We sit
on the grass in the sun and eat cold chicken and ham,
salad and plum pudding. Get back for tea to find that
Dua had called leaving a wreath for N and I and some
fruit, which was probably the *most* touching gift of all.
My bearer presented me with a wreath too, so my room
now quite a bower of flowers. Dine with N and return
to my room at 9.30.

Boxing Day 1952
A quiet day at the Seminar and early to bed.

27th December 1952, *Saturday*
Go to see a Czech children's film in the evening. A puppet film in colours of an old fairy story. Quite enchanting and a real work of art. Scenery, costumes and the
puppets based on mediaeval pictures and beautifully
done, with no vulgarity. An idealogical twist at the end
when the hero returns with his princess bride to his

father's cottage instead of living happily for ever more
in the castle. The most memorable characters the old
king and the jester.

28th December 1952, *Sunday*

Quiet day in my room reading. Visited by sellers of
Kashmiri jewellery and am persuaded to buy some
trinkets at four times their proper value.

To Kotah House in evening (dinner jacket). A
celebration to raise money for the children of the servants. Games, fork supper, dancing Paul Jones, etc.,
and singing. Doris and Bill much to the fore. Get home
about 1.00.

29 December 1952, *Monday*

Cash cheque at bank. Norman gives a most interesting
talk on the Scientific Classification of Colour which for
most of the time completely bored many of the students. However he made most of them understand by
the end which was a real achievement. On the way
home N and I visit Miss Kanaka's room at her school
to see her pictures. One or two nice watercolours. The
room interesting as an example of an Indian maiden
lady's establishment. Some books (Bernard Shaw), a
clutter of boxes and cooking materials, a big guitar and
a bed. Miss K bright and pretty, Southern Indian. The
usual tale of woe. I fear she is a troublemaker.

Take all Jeswamis out to dinner. Mrs and Miss look
extremely pretty in their best clothes. Have an idea they
were somewhat disappointed at the Maiden's Hotel.
Should have taken them somewhere smarter. Gaylord's
or Wenger's.

made most of them understand by the end
which was a real achievement. On the
way home N. to visit Miss Kane's room at

30th December 1952, *Tuesday*

The silk screen won't work. See Biswas on way home who promises some material. Quiet evening writing letters.

31st December 1952, *Wednesday*

Afternoon off. Go to bed early.

1st January 1953, *Thursday*

A holiday. With N entertain some of the photographic trainees and have my photograph taken. Enormous M[oral] R[earmament] party in the dining room. So many 'nice' women with indeterminate faces and dowdy hats. Like a vicarage tea party. Good young men with large Adam's apples.

Take Louise Birkett and N out to dinner at the Volga. Nice but expensive.

2nd January 1953, *Friday*

Develop a feverish cold and go to bed early with aspirin.

3rd January 1953, *Saturday*

Stay in bed till tea. The bed hard and many disturbances — sweeper, seller of Kashmiri goods, the postman and stray bearers. Glad to get up at 5.00, feeling unpleasant but convalescent. Visited by Kedar Nath.

4th January 1953, *Sunday*

Pick up Haq, Jaimal and Miss Kanaka at Jamia Milia. Lunch by a wide stretch of water formed by the Jumna River and into which the Agra Canal enters by means of big lock gates. The ground by the lock shaded by big trees and a favourite picnic place for Delhi citizens on holidays. A line of small open air restaurants in sunken ground — balloon sellers. Big crowd round the snake charmer but did not have time to stay and see him in

action. Feel much better but tired. A sort of sub cold.

5th January 1953, Monday

Try printing ink through the silk screen and it works.
What a relief. Miss Lila Sen and another lady from
UNESCO call upon us. Pleased that they find us all
hard at work. Taken to an exhibition of Delhi Artists'
Society. Miserable show. Very amateurish works, bad-
ly framed and hung in a dark, cold hall hung with gun-
ny sacks. Find it difficult to make even polite noises.
Drive back in a tonga and arrive frozen.

6th January 1953, Tuesday

Cold and grey again. Continue to have a sore throat.
Busy day at Seminar. Shop silk, printing inks and tools
in Chandni Chowk and Chawri Bazaar.

Visited by another Kashmiri seller of embroidered
woollens, etc. and strong-mindedly buy nothing. Dine
at Gaylord's with Norman. Expensive but quite good
Chinese food. Two very pretty Indian girls at the next
table.

7th January 1953, Wednesday

See a puppet show in the morning. The puppeteers — a
man, wife and small boy (with an assistant unseen) from
Rajasthan. The show, am told by Indians, not very
good but I found it entrancing. They had the sadness
of a Daumier drawing. The man played the drum and
spoke the talking parts. The woman and boy sang behind the scenes, while the assistant, behind the scenes
too, manipulated the puppets. The puppet characters
mostly kings and princes. The comic character a drum-
mer who undergoes much knocking about by the court

Puppeteers visit to the photographed by in film & phot. boys —

chamberlain but always pops up to drum again — a Mr
Punch character. The puppeteers as sad and ragged and
quiet that seemed to suggest the very quintessence of
that melancholy that one associates with the unsuccess-
ful show business.

8th January 1953, Thursday

Make a mess of the small silk screen again. Fear it will
never work. I can't stretch the silk tight enough. The
silk stretches and bulges after it has been in use. See
young man in evening with idea for film scenario.
Puppeteers visit to be photographed by the film and
photo boys.

9th January 1953, Friday

Quiet day at Seminar.

10th January 1953, Saturday

Norman gives a film show in the morning. His own
and other various types of animated film. Lunch at the
Madras with N and Miss Kanaka. The woman becoming a bit of a menace and she quarrels with the other
trainees and hangs round N and me. Move my room
suddenly to 107. My bearer lays on a bathroom with
an Indonesian gentleman. Buy myself some gin and
Dubonnet.

Take Bill and Doris to Gaylord's where we have
a not too expensive Chinese meal.

11th January 1953, Sunday

Sit indoors all day. Write, doodle and practise stereo-
scopic doodles.

12th January 1953, Monday

The little screen seems to work. Alas, Thakur rips the

Friday 9th quiet day & lemon...

Saturday 10 Norman
gave a film show in
the morning. His own &
other various types of
animated film...
...tion Lunch at ...
Madras with N. & Mrs
Kanak. The woman becoming
a bit of a menace & she
quarrels with ... all
the... & hangs round
N. & I. Move my room
Suddenly to 107. My
Brian hangs on an army
of porters. To share a
bathroom with an Indonesian
gentleman. Buy myself
some gin. Dubonnet.
Take Bill & Doris to Jaylords
where we have a not too expensive Chinese meal

screen in washing it. See the film and photo strips made
by trainees in the afternoon. .

13th January 1953, *Tuesday*
Busy day at the Seminar. Shukla and others visit. To see
a show of pictures at the Feemasons' Hall. Two artists,
the work of one not unpleasant and refreshing to see.
Have asked him round to tea.

N and I take five trainees who sleep at the Institute
out to dinner at the Madras. Shrivastava his usual
buoyant self. The dinner I think a great success.

14th January 1953, *Wednesday*
Haq's drawing on the small silk screen a sufficient success to encourage us to start on the big screen. Kalam
visits us from Jamia Milia and gives us some tips. Visits
too by Pires and a UNESCO chap. A very active day for
both Norman and me. Great thunderstorms which
lasted all night. My bowl fire fuses.

15th January 1953, *Thursday*
Morning grey and ground drenched with rain. Hus-
saini, artist who has made our sandals, turns up at the
Seminar. Grey and more rain during [day]. Return to
Constitution House in another great thunderstorm and
torrents of rain. Sorry [for] the poor refugees in their
straw huts. The ones near the Seminar swamped last
night.

16th January 1953, *Friday*
Sun comes out mid morning and warms us all up.

17th January 1953, *Saturday*
A rather hectic morning at the school. My big screen
with its glue stencil quite floppy and useless indoors, but
rigid when out in the sun. It looks as if the glue was very

sensitive to moisture. Waste a lot of paint in trying to mix up the first colours.

18th January 1953, Sunday

Kirmani takes me out on the back of his motorcycle to see a village. The village, a large one, situated partly within the walls of an old fort beside a shallow stream with high steep banks. In the village, low buildings and winding footways with runnels of deep mud or muddy water in the centre of them. A few wider places with big stone walls and large trees. Animals and children in profusion. Black oxen, camels resting on the ground. Dogs, many puppies, and donkeys. Women wearing brilliant clothes. Men sitting about playing cards. Women at the wells and children of all ages, from half-naked toddlers to teenagers. All muddy to look at. It was as if the mud had got inextricably mixed up with the animals and humanity to make a sort of living mud pie.

19th January 1953, Monday

N in bed with sore throat. A terrible day at the Institute with silk screen troubles. Fear it will never work in the time at our disposal. Only four weeks now.

20th January 1953, Tuesday

Much as before. Sit up late working out a talk on lettering — the blind leading the blind.

21st January 1953, Wednesday

Visit by Saiyid Din and Shukla in the morning. Dua poster an irretrievable flop, but not unproductive as see possibilities in using cut stencil with the screen. See Czech film *The Emperor's Nightingale* with N and trainees. Film not as good as the first puppet film seen last month but beautiful all the same. With N dine Dua and Ganguli.

22nd January 1953, *Thursday*

Quiet day at the Institute preparatory to the next attempt on the silk screen. The calm before the storm. Tea with Saiyid Din, gathering of high-up civil servants. Young women beautiful but tremendous Blue Stockings. A frivolous or flirtatious remark unthinkable. They are clever and amusing, however. Refused the cake which I was told afterwards was a very rude thing to do.

P.S. Shopped in the Chawri Bazaar in the morning and now realise that I did not see anything. How blind one is when one is not thinking. The Artist's job of noticing is a whole time one otherwise one loses so much.

P.S. to Thursday — Ganguli taken sick.

23rd January 1953, *Friday*

Ganguli in hospital. All of us vaccinated in case of smallpox. N very tired and not at all well.

Work with Haq on the silk screen stencil. Dua very upset and distraught about the spoiling of his poster. Visit Ganguli at the fever hospital. Obviously only has chicken pox.

24th January 1953, *Saturday*

Morning at the Seminar. A hoped for afternoon of work disturbed by Miss Kanaka and Haq.

25th January 1953, *Sunday*

Mass early, then to Central Institute and draw design for Certificate on plate. Drawing goes down well. To Kohtah's house in evening and see a show put on chiefly

P.S. to Thursday — Ganguli taken sick
Friday 23 . Ganguli in Hospital — All of us
must vaccinated — can be has small pox.

N. very timid & not at all well.
Work with Hay on it till leaves blowing .
Was very upset & obstinate about it opening of
his pictures — Visit Ganguli at it
fever hospital — obviously only has Chicken. pox .

by children. 'All dresses made by Doris.

26th January 1953, *Monday*

Independence Day. Curzon Road full of people on foot
and in tongas streaming to the route of the procession.
Many peasant women in their best clothes of brilliant
materials. Take a taxi to the Institute to make our way
through the throng. Long day at the Institute producing
a lithograph by hand rolling — no press. Quite a
success and looks a possible medium for cheap local
production of printed matter. At first attempt over 100
prints in the day. Should treble this output with prac-
tice.

27th January 1953, *Tuesday*

Second colour doesn't go on so well. Maybe the wrong
consistency of ink. All the students around too asking
damn silly questions. Far more tiring day in consequence, though half the work produced. To tea with
Bose and his family. A much warmer day with thunder
and rain in the early morning. Sit up till 2.00 writing
notes.

28th January 1953, *Wednesday*

To the Stadium in the evening to see Indian folk dancing. A vast arena and the stage a little too far away to see
the performers clearly. However some interesting dancing. Most memorable were the tall men in white caps
and gowns with long white drums dancing an accompaniment, and also men in white dancing with drawn
swords. The tribal war dance of the Indo-Africans
spectacular too.

29th January 1953, *Thursday*

To the UK High Commission and get my passport re-

Wednesday 28. To the Stadium in
the evening to see Indian Folk dancing.
A vast arena & the stage a little too
far away to see the performers clearly.
However some interesting dancing.
Most memorable were the tall men in
white caps & gowns with long white
drums dancing an accompaniment.
& also men in white dancing with drawn
swords. The tribal war dances of Indo-African
spectacular too.

Thursday 29th
To the U.K. High Commission
& get my passport renewed,
shop look in Chandni chowk.
& visit I.C.I. office
collect samples paint —
then tomorrow over to tea
with -? Singh - Shukla & Mr
~

the car & I have the students' bicycle to consider.

I write my deposition —

newed. Shop silk in Chandni Chowk and visit ICI office
to collect sample paints. After Seminar over to tea with
Singh, Shukla and N. Discuss opening of Adult Education Centre. Back at 7.15 and settle down to write when
visited by Kanaka. Dine out with N.

30th January 1953, Friday
Some successful (seemingly) experiments with colours
for the silk screen. Hectic time trying to give individual
attention to so many students. Sam arrives at Seminar to
say that my room has been burgled. Visit Ganguli at the
fever hospital. Shrivastava shows his arm to the doctor.
Badly infected. Get home to find the thief has taken
Narian's bicycle, my half-hunter watch, dinner suit and,
according to Sam, some shirts and socks. Obviously an
inside job, as my room the only one with no bolt at the
bottom of the back door. Sam naturally implicated —
all rather horrible. Would gladly have done nothing but
the loss of Narian's bicycle made it imperative to call in
the police. The police — a fat sergeant and two assis-
tants — pleasant but not seemingly efficient. This may
be due to lack of knowledge on my part. They come
tomorrow to take finger prints of the back door but I
know they are already covered with prints from Sam's
fingers, the fat man from down the block and mine. The
fat man quite ghoulish, like an old woman at a street
accident. Would like Sam to be led away in chains.

Have to visit the Maharana [?]. Find her looking like
a fine odalisque reclining in bed with a cold.

To dinner at the Maiden's Hotel. Our host, Evelyn
Wood. Other guest pretty and intelligent woman
attaché from USA Embassy.

31st January 1953, Saturday

Measured for my suit. Sam's aged mother and friend
call on me at Institute. The old lady in great distress.
Sam taken to police station for questioning. She says
he will be beaten up. Only fear it is true and feel awful,
though helpless, about it. I mustn't interfere as the
police will trump up the case and I have the student's
bicycle to consider. I write my deposition. Sam back
in evening in great state of indignation at being questioned. Go to the police station where I am promised he
won't be 'harassed' — a queer word. Sam to report
back at 9.00 tomorrow.

1st February 1953, Sunday

A day out with N and Gopal. We visit the Red Fort.
Lunch at Moti Mahal's and I make drawings at the foot
of the Masjid Mosque. Finish up by visiting the solar-
ium. Get back to find a deputation of Sam's mother and
his brother-in-law. Sam's mother in great distress as
Sam not returned from police station. With N to the
police station where we were told the Inspector and Sam
had left. However, just leaving when Sam dashed out.
See the Inspector, take Sam away with us but promise
to return him at 8 this evening to be questioned for three
hours and then sent home. Sam in a great state of terror,
in fear of being beaten up. N and I feel awful but helpless. 9.30 Sam back with his mother, both beaming.
Seems the Inspector only questioned him shortly and
then dismissed him. Thank heaven. My stock very
much up, as Sam thinks his quick release all my doing.

2nd February 1953, Monday

Pleasant dinner party with the McInnes. Meet Shankar

233

of *Shankar's Weekly*. Dinner lavish, including whisky, a
white burgundy, brandy and rum. I fear it would make
an ardent Wine and Food Society member shudder but I
enjoyed myself.

3rd February 1953, *Tuesday*
Visit some rather fascinating back streets behind Chandni Chowk on a shopping expedition.

4th February 1953, *Wednesday*
Shrivastava and trainees living at the Institute give us a
dinner cooked by themselves in their quarters. Much
photographed by flashlight. Food excellent, prepared by
our youngest trainee. A dormitory meal. All very
merry.

5th February 1953, *Thursday*
An easier day at the Seminar. Visit Shankar of *Shankar's
Weekly* on the way home and delighted but exhausted
by seeing a great number of children's paintings from
his exhibitions. The big Turkish ones quite remarkably
beautiful.

Taken to dinner given by Mr Wilson, T[he]
C[ultural] A[ttaché], and wife. Heart sank a little when
entered the room. Two elderly Trots, man and wife,
who concoct children's books which sell 500,000 at a
time. American, needless to say. Hostess also concocts
children's books, an efficient Austrian woman. Eat dinner off our knees. Look at coloured photos of Bali.

6th February 1953, *Friday*
Stop near the Mori Gate on the way to Seminar and visit
a chemical shop. Interesting place, dim and full of bottles and strange glass apparatus for chemistry. The

approach to the shop through a courtyard (secretive looking) and cluttered with baled and packed goods. Odd doors and stairways lead off to strange and unmentionable quarters. Here one seems to have to penetrate the deepest and most sinister slum warrens to reach the traders' establishments. Always they are difficult to find.

7th February 1953, Saturday
Screen giving trouble. Find kerosene beginning to rot the black rubber of our big squeegee. Unending problems. Leave Seminar late. Lunch at the Madras with N and spend the rest of the day in room, reading instead of working.

8th February 1953, Sunday
Day in my room making a drawing for *Vogue*.[6]

9th February 1953, Monday
Say goodbye to the fat man at our table. Heavy day at the Institute. Get some good prints off Dua's plate of which I had despaired. The silk screen progresses fairly favourably. Find glassiate pencils a good substitute for chalk. Get home late and tired to find Kanaka installed. More than I can bear. However N takes her in tow and discusses her work. Have a laryngitis cough.

10th February 1953, Tuesday
We at last produce a poster by silk screen. Technically, alas, a rather third-rate product but it's something. Shukla visits us in the afternoon. Taken by Kedar Nath to his home for a sort of high tea. Air of great impoverishment. One dismal room for him, his wife and four children. An old blue cotton curtain screening off one end where his wife was cooking. The meal produced, all

237

in little dishes, was delicious. The wife very pretty and the children sweet.

11*th February* 1953, *Wednesday*
Another exhausting day at the Institute. The new poster promises well. Get back late to find the tailor has [made] a mess of my drill trousers. To bed early when I should have been thinking of my lecture on Sunday.

12*th February* 1953, *Thursday*
Silk screen printing of Nippur Rey's poster in full swing with its attendant alarms due to bad paint, register, etc. Take Louise Birkett, N, out to dinner of strange chicken dish which did not taste of anything very much.

13*th February* 1953, *Friday*
A pleasant day shopping with Doris. Lunch on Chinese food at Gaylord's, and reading and writing in my room. Feel much better.

Visit Mrs Wasi to advise about a cover design for UN-ESCO pamphlet. Hear a diatribe against my little design for Certificate — 'Terrible eye, ghastly ear. Frightfully English, only stopped it being used just in time.' Attempted to confess but as she wouldn't believe that I had anything to do with it I gave up the attempt. Silly cow.

Madiah Gowda dines with us at Constitution House.

14*th February* 1953, *Saturday*
Find my silk screen boys have worked like galley slaves and finished Nippur Rey's poster, and done it well too. Both delighted and touched. At the Institute till 6.00, writing reports and talking to Shukla. Return to Constitution House with a bumping in my ears and feeling exhausted. N and I put rum in our tea and just begin-

ning to feel refreshed when Miss Kanaka arrives. Maddening. One can never get away from the students.

I distrust Shukla, a bland minor official. Hear from him the grand and pompous plans for a Certificate-giving ceremony, with the Minister in the chair. Will probably have to give a speech. More work and so unnecessary.

N arrives back rather shattered to say that he has had a violent proposal of marriage from K. We dine out on the strength of it. Before this happens, however, visited by eight elderly, bearded Sikhs. The eldest old villain of them introduced as Dr Sant Sind, PhD London. Discover after some time they are begging for charity, probably rather bogus.

15th February 1953, Sunday

All day in my room sweating up lecture for Catholic Action Society. Arrive to find epidiascope did not work. The audience, about fifteen, arrived three quarters of an hour late (Benediction was late). Made the best job I could of an illustrated lecture without illustrations. Seven of the audience had no clue as to my theme. Feel rather sore. Am sufficiently eminent and also too busy to be inflicted with this sort of thing. A horrid waste. These Catholic Societies are quite immoral.

16th February 1953, Monday

Norman ill. Phone for a doctor before leaving. Find silk screen boys getting on well. Surprisingly enough not too busy a day at Seminar and could work on written matter. Return to find N suffering from dysentery (maybe amoebic). Sit up late writing notes for cyclostyling.

17th February 1953, *Tuesday*

Tiring day at the Seminar. Get back to find N better but has amoebic dysentery which is serious. Shrivastava, Bora, Biswas, Miss Kanaka and finally Gowda visit him. A horde which was bad for him and exhausting for me. Bright spot, Thakur's silk screen poster the best printed so far.

18th February 1953, *Wednesday*

Alone to Seminar. Organise cleaning up parties. Back to Constitution House to hear that N has to go into hospital for at least a fortnight — a frightful blow. Return with Bora to Seminar, lunchless. See a man from Bangalore interested in silk screen printing. Dash off a drawing for a catalogue cover. 4.30 — 6.00 preside at a conference of local publishers and printers. 6.30 — 7.00 in conference with N and Shukla about future plans. Late tea with Pires and back to Constitution House half dead. But N a really sick man and worse.

19th February 1953, *Thursday*

Another gruelling day, but things beginning to take shape. Norman's lunch a grand affair. Servants in white with purple stripes in their turbans. *Pilau*, etc — though a poor feast without him. TCA (Wilson) calls. See film strips. Call on N at the hospital on way back. Two very large gins with Louise Birkett. Take Doris and Bill out to dinner and forget my troubles for a brief two hours.

20th February 1953, *Friday*

All day at work designing our Exhibition plus a hundred and one other details to attend to. By the Grace of God the Exhibition begins to look well. Students' tea at 4.30, after which I have to make a speech. Visit N on way back with Shukla. Then police station where I find my watch and dinner jacket. The latter cut down to suit a smaller man, so useless. Back very late and try and concoct my vote of thanks to the Minister for Ed. tomorrow.

21st February 1953, Saturday

The great day is over and I feel it has been some sort of success, but all my doing. The ineptitude of Hussain, the idle stupidity of Das and the crises that have blown up! I have bullied, contrived, cajoled, and worked like a maniac. I have given our set speech and half-a-dozen extempore ones to large audiences and now, thank God, it is ended. All the wrong people have been awarded at least with kindness. The M. of Ed. was phoned and the Ministry also, so all is well. Galviya touched my heart when he said good-bye. I was moved.

Shrivastava play not so good — he is a real ham actor — overplayed everything.

22nd February 1953, Sunday

Mass. See N and spend the rest of the day rather lazily writing and reading.

23rd February 1953, Monday

Day packing up at the Seminar, winding up with a last talk on Practical Perspective. See N on the way back. Ganguli and Nippur Rey with me. We drink rum and discuss art and my work.

24th February 1953, Tuesday

Wonderful to be away from the Seminar and feel that it is now all over. See N, read and write letters, do accounts, etc. Still lots to do, alas.

25th February 1953, *Wednesday*

Make mistake of going to the Customs House myself to see through the tubes of work for UNESCO and *Vogue*. Spent hours there. Leave the *Vogue* package for Cox & Kings to deal with. See N and Murray. A pleasant lunch with Doris and Bill. Go and look at the paintings by Dr Fabri and his Indian wife. Wish he didn't wear a wig.

26th February 1953, *Thursday*

To police station. Wait in magistrate's court as I am witness in robbery case. However, case did not come on owing to prisoner's counsel engaged in another case. Back to court in afternoon and in the witness stand. Counsel for defence try to suggest that goods not mine and could be bought in the bazaar. Proceedings not finished so have to attend court tomorrow. Get caught by an elderly Catholic woman with hard luck story and sorrowfully part with 10 rupees.

27th February 1953, *Friday*

Morning shopping. 2.30 to court to find proceedings postponed to about 3.30. Hang about at court from 3.30 – 4.00, when write note to magistrate who allows me to collect my things. No more cross-examination in the witness stand which was a relief. To tea at Jamia Milia and back by 6.30. Miss K calls in and as N won't speak to her a little distressing. Get rid of the impossible creature as kindly as possible. Bill and Doris arrive for drinks. Dinner at Constitution House.

28th February 1953, *Saturday*

All day packing. Very hot and bright outside so remain quietly indoors. Sam tries on my dinner jacket which now being cut down suits him to a tee. He is delighted.

always with the peachy hills in the
distance. Cross over a great area of the sea.
the through suburbs with many
been to arrive at Bombay at about 9.00.
Find port. Hostel with some difficulty. Have
a large room with balcony facing the sea.
Sit in my room, draw & sort out notes of
toto I do till lunch time.

1st March 1953, *Sunday*

Leave Delhi station at 8.00 for Bombay. N, Sam and Jeswami see me off. Share a compartment with an Army officer. Till lunch through flat, formless country. Very dry though some pretty villages. All poor and peasants on stations and by the wayside stained with coloured powder or water. Holi[7]. Lunch in dining car. Return to carriage. Gangapur[?] a dusty looking place in an even dustier plain. The desert of Rajasthan. Sandy, covered with scrub and very hot. A few tiny villages seemingly of straw, herds of goats. Women in red clothes, men often with red turbans. The inside of our carriage full of dust.

2nd March 1953, *Monday*

Wake at dawn to find oneself in new country. A range of hills feathered with trees in the distance, waterways and tall palms in the foreground. Pass mile after mile of salt pans, always with the feathery hills in the distance. Cross over a great arm of the sea, then through suburbs with many trees to arrive at Bombay at about 9.00. Find Govt. Hostel with some difficulty. Have a large room with balcony facing the sea. Sit in my room, draw and sort out notes of jobs to do till lunchtime.

Note: Some pools dry and being stamped by workmen. Bigger causeways with heaps of salt and an occasional shack or two.

Afternoon shopping with clerk from the Min. of Ed. branch office here. Decidedly hot, sweat in shirt and trousers only.

3rd March 1953, *Tuesday*

Very hot night. Sit on my balcony before sunrise and watch the early morning walkers on the esplanade. Go shopping again with the silly ass. Fix up for paint and litho materials fairly satisfactorily. Back to Oceanic for lunch. A cool sea breeze has brought the temperature down. Norman turns up. We shop together in the afternoon.

4th March 1953, *Wednesday*

Morning shopping. Leave Bombay by 8.10 train. Some spectacular country at sunset. Mountainous with deep ravines and forests. Poona at 8.30 and change trains. Great crowds of Indians in family parties squatting on the dim platform. Porters in scarlet jackets and turbans. N and I each have coupé to ourselves. Disturbed night with many stops.

5th March 1953, *Thursday*

Early morning through open country and then through a land of well-tilled fields, fine great trees (English parkland), rich red earth. Green things growing and more solidly built cottages. Most grateful to the eye. A country with form — rivers, dams, fort on a hill, long saddle-backed downs. Drop down to Belgaum, richer country still. Bright red earth. A great moated wall, some old fortifications. Women in dark purples and greens carrying copper pots. Fine-looking draught cattle. From Belgaum to Londa. Forests, dry brake. Bamboo and arcas like wooded valleys in Kent, though no green grass. Arrive Hubli after traversing a high plateau. Open country, wide fields, cotton. Four hour halt at Hubli where we lunch in the train. Stay in train as too hot outside. Leave Hubli at 7.10. Cross a wide plain. Neat, pretty villages. Beautifully-made haystacks. Clean and tidy fields of great size. Cotton, etc. Threshing floors, etc, all spick and span. Red earth. Pretty, neat stations with platforms lined with oak trees.

6th March 1953, *Friday*

Arrive Bangalore at dawn. Nobody to meet us. Go to Hindu Hotel and hire room with bath, etc, to change and wash.

Meet Adult Ed. chaps. Buy paper at Colvani's. See Govt. printing works. Excellent lunch at hotel. Other guests eating off palm leaves. See director Govt. printing press at 4.15, not very helpful. Leave Bangalore at 5.10. Arrive [Mysore] at 10.30 and are taken to an hotel.

7th March 1953, *Saturday*

In the morning visit Wesley Press. Meet very pleasant English printer there — may be most useful. After lunch, during which we met Wilson of TCA, visit the venue of the Seminar. Splendid 1840 bungalow, Palladian style with central portico and curving passages to wings. Inside still some fine furniture left. Chandeliers in linen bags, a few sofas and good chairs. Also a few 17th- and early 18th-century pictures (sporting) in very bad condition. But place magnificently spacious with still remnants of the Grand Manner. Full of nostalgic charm. Around, a laid out park with big mango, tamarind and other trees. Fine views over surrounding country. Arid country. Earth all shades of red, dotted with green trees and some palms but not many. Many peasants on the road. The women small and dark and

Much talk about the arrangements of the
Samāj — At dinner try some of the
local Toddy — quite filthy.

Monday 9th — Leave Hassan in morning
day at the Bungalow settling off. Will
N. Badriah & Sriniwasan of Mysore in evening
Visit Hostel Keeper & his Sanatorium. din—

Wednesday 11th Gowder & other visitors in
morning. Support to be small-medium in it
learning clumped. lots now back
& no work.... My son at
last time. meet a number of
journalists - N. & I have
to speak a few words - Show
of Film ships
Then to village
see a drama being rehearsed. Seated
in a close ring of villagers - children on the floor

mostly wearing dark saris. Deep purple, greens and indigo. Cattle small and elegant with long horns. Stop and drink the milk from a fresh coconut on the return journey to Mysore.

8th March 1953, *Sunday*

Late at 7.00 Mass as the tonga driver takes me miles out of the way to a Scotch Presbyterian Mission church by mistake. The bulk of the congregation at Mass squatting on the floor. The women in their best saris on the left of the aisle, the men on the right. A very pretty sight. Shukla turns up early. Visit with him and Norman the vegetable, fruit and general merchandise market. An enchanting place of deep shadows and vivid colours. Splendid looking vegetables. After lunch visit our bungalow again. Much talk about the arrangement of the Seminar. At dinner try some of the local toddy. Quite filthy.

9th March 1953, *Monday*

Leave hotel in morning. Day at the bungalow settling in. With N, Badriah and Srinivasin to Mysore in evening. Visit Hotel Keeper in his sanctum. Drink pineapple juice and eat titbits. Then shop. Mosquito nets, a torch, some rum and a pretty object for Nicky.[8] Mysore a pretty little town. Nice, clean, bright shops. Shukla buys diamonds. Back late to Seminar and find chaos still reigns. Lots still being fitted up and latrines yet to be dug.

10th March 1953, *Tuesday*

In the evening visit a nearby village. Lovely valley, three wells. Dark women in darker saris walking up the hill with copper pots on their heads. A village man accompanies us. He had a beautiful face — like a fawn, delicate little nose, sharp beady eyes and hair growing down low over his forehead and tufts of hair on cheeks and chin. See a village outdoor film show arranged by the M[ysore] S[tate] A[dult] E[ducation] C[ouncil].

11 *March 1953, Wednesday*

Gowda and others visit us in morning. Subject to be dealt with in the Seminar changed. Lots more talk and no work. Mysore at tea time. Meet a number of journalists. N and I have to speak a few words. Show of film strips. Then to village to see a drama being rehearsed, seated in a close ring of villagers, children on the floor, men standing. The actors, all men, stood and recited or sung to an harmonium. Faces in the lamplight very beautiful.

12*th March 1953, Thursday*

After tea walk to a nearby village, Srinivasin with me. Sit under a tree and make a drawing. Walk home slowly in the dusk. Cry of a leopard from the forest to our left which set all the birds chattering.

13*th March 1953, Friday*

Problems caused by financial difficulties of our students. They can't pay the caterer. Afternoon in my room drawing and writing. The usual twilight but alas too short. All the trainees off as it is half day. N, Hussain and myself have the place to ourselves, which is delightful. Rat hunt in N's room.

14*th March 1953, Saturday*

A holiday. To Mysore in the morning. Cash cheque, shop, lunch at the Metropole. In the afternoon visit the Maharaja's Palace. A monument of Indo-Victorian vul-

'A Road in Mysore State, India' (10½ × 14½), signed EA, 1953, Private collection, Kent. Reproduced by kind permission of the owner. Photograph by Nicholas Ardizzone.

garity. Bad, over-ornate Indian architecture, gold and silver thrones, statuettes from England, circa 1880, and stuffed tigers. Four old doors in silver and ivory. Bas reliefs (bawdy ones) the only exception. In the evening by the council van to some celebrated gardens[9] under the big dam about seven and a half miles out of town. The gardens not at their best, as many of the fountains and artificial falls not working owing to the lowness of the water. However, pretty enough when lit up. Some lovely groups of Indians eating their supper by the water's edge. Back at the bungalow to find that two of the trainees had cut their fingers badly with broken glass. Send them into hospital by the van. Galviya arrived.

15th March 1953, *Sunday*

Unpack Delhi goods in morning. Trainees at work on silk screen in afternoon. Much dissatisfaction with conditions shown by some of the trainees.

16th March 1953, *Monday*

More or less a holiday here as it is New Year's Day for these parts. Visit by Badriah and others. In the evening determined to stay behind and write and draw, find myself alone in bungalow. However, drumming and singing from nearby village proved irresistible so walked over to it and arrived at last light. A procession in progress. A silver affair representing Rama, Sita and Lakshman and some god, the whole surmounted by red umbrella carried round by four men on poles. A Brahmin, naked to the waist, being the officiating priest in front. The procession led by trumpeters, blowing serpents, and drummers. Long line of people, men, women and children lying in the roadway so that the

procession could pass over them. Procession halted at each cottage, where midst tremendous cheering the housewife would make an offering of a coconut split in half laid on a brass tray and lit by a tiny oil lamp. My arrival set all the dogs barking and the women giggling. However, I was soon taken in tow by a responsible male and surrounded by a milling crowd of men and children following the procession. At one point I was offered bananas, and when, taking two, I said *'Saccu'* (enough) I was cheered to the echo. I think they looked on me as a good omen for the New Year, like a dark man crossing the threshold. With difficulty I explained that I was English, not American, and was answered by shouts of 'Ingelu'. 'U' is added to most English words, such as ink bottellu, soapsu, etc.

17*th March* 1953, *Tuesday*

No supplies yet. N and I give lectures. Badriah, Narayan, Bose, Suleman turn up in the evening, the former with supplies. A large party in our room.

18*th March* 1953, *Wednesday*

The art wing begins to look like a printing shop which fills one with hope. Into Mysore with N and Srinivasin after tea. Buy liquor. Meet Badriah and others. Back in time for dinner.

19*th March* 1953, *Thursday*

Visit by McInnes at breakfast time. Busy day. Experiment with glue glycerine. Design poster. Tirmani, Gowda and Narayan here after tea.

20*th March* 1953, *Friday*

Experiment with glue stencil in morning. Quiet afternoon, being a half holiday, at work designing a bill and poster. N arrives back from Mysore with the news that we may have to leave — cause water shortage.

21st March 1953, Saturday

A party of us — Norman and I, Hussain and wife, to be taken by Badriah to a village the other side of the big dam, to see folk dancing. Items — stick dancing, dancing to drums. A well-known musician playing on a wind instrument and some solo turns, all by men. After show watch a short religious procession. Statues of the gods (hidden by artificial flowers, etc) carried round in a lighted palanquin to the beating of drums and piping of pipes. Later we all dined in the head man's house. Back rather late. A fascinating evening. (Note the great wooden triumphal car elaborately carved with erotic designs.)

22nd March 1953, Sunday

Mass in morning and breakfast with Badriah afterwards. Into Mysore during day to see our proposed new quarters in an exhibition building. My heart in my boots when I see it. Like working in a hospital.

I doubt if water shortage is as acute as is made out, but pressure coming from our Indian profs and others who are town birds and want the urban amenities. Blast them all.

Visit a village late afternoon. Party of us try a track through the forest. See the *machan*[10] for the leopard and turn back when nearly at our goal, so arrive late. The village headman interviewed.

23rd March 1953, Monday

Attempt to engrave wax stones a failure. Wax too thick. Evening in bungalow working.

Saturday 21st. A party of us – Alamin & b.
Hussain & wife ... taken by Badier & a
village on other side of the Big Dam, to see
folk dancing. ... – Stick dancing,
dancing to drums – A well known Musician playing
on it a wind instrument & some solo turns all
by men. After show watched a short
religious procession – Statues of the god (buried
by artificial flowers etc.) carried round in a
lighted palanquin to the beating of drums
& piping of pipers. Later we all dined in
the head man's house. Back rather late.
A fascinating evening. (Note the great
wooden triumphal car elaborately carved
with erotic designs.)

24th March 1953, *Tuesday*

First colour of Dua's poster printed on the ss. Not too good. Stay in in evening and start redrawing on wax. Water crisis. Narayan here in evening. Discussion about payment of bills, water and other matters.

25th March 1953, *Wednesday*

In evening with N, Badriah and Srinivasin to Sriranga-patam. Have a look at a delightful house by the river as a possible place for Seminar. Alas, catering difficulties make it impractical. Visit Tipu Sultan's[11] summer palace. Delightful frescoes. One, a battle scene, T's troops including French soldiers attacking Wellesley's troops, who are in a hollow square. The latter obviously getting the worst of it.

Late back and tired, but find Haq, Tandon and Abyan Khan had provided a dish of meat from the nearby village, so have a sort of dormitory feast in N's and my room. Two bottles beer and half bottle of my rum consumed.

26th March 1953, *Thursday*

Very busy day printing second colour of Dua's poster. Ganguli arrives.

27th March 1953, *Friday*

Half day, though busy on engraving wax and preparing for next silk screen colour.

28th March 1953, *Saturday*

Mysore with Dr and Mrs Hussain in morning. Afternoon at work in room.

29th March 1953, *Sunday*

First poster printed. Tusche method a success, thank heaven. Still too many faults through carelessness. In evening to see a show of folk art in Mysore.

Very noisy due to loud speakers not rehearsed enough. Heartily bored.

30th March 1953, Monday

John Bowers arrives. In evening he, N and I, with one or two trainees, visit the nearest village and start the villagers drawing on large sheets of paper with coloured chalks. Offered prizes for best work, and induced some of the women to join the competition. The latter would not draw in the open. One sixteen-year-old seemed to show some talent. Asked him to come up to the class. Father doubtful, as he had work to do. Approaching thunder storm and wild wind add movement and bustle in the village. Group of small boys playing trains.

31st March 1953, Tuesday

Frustrated morning due to the wrong paint being ordered. JB leaves us after lunch. Into Mysore shopping with N, the Hussains and Ganguli. Usual boredom of going about with a party.

1st April 1953, Wednesday

Complete washout on silk screens. About fifteen rupees worth of paint wasted.

2nd April 1953, Thursday

Most of the day spent in Mysore shopping, on the whole successfully.

3rd April 1953, Friday

Disastrous day with the silk screen. Everything went wrong that could go wrong.

4th April 1953, Saturday

Some successful prints. Into Mysore to shop, etc. Come back to find Ganguli and N had finished the rum. Towards dusk a first hint of rain. Wonderful stormy sun-

Thursday 2nd

Most of the day spent
in Mysore shopping
on the whole
successfully.

set, great rainbow. Flashes of lightning.

5th April 1953, *Sunday*

To Mysore in early morning. Breakfast at the Metropole. Seminar by 9.00. Dua's second colour goes on well. Visit by Eagleton accompanied by Badriah and others. Temperature much cooler owing to rain in the neighbourhood, though no rain here. Cloudy sky which makes country look very much like England. A productive day. Air India tell me that they can book my flight for the 30th.

6th April 1953, *Monday*

Das makes a horrible mistake in silk screen stencil which delays proceeding. Theoretical talk by Hussain. Another spectacular evening with a storm of rain, thunder and lightning, and a spectacular evening sky. Landscape like a pre-Raphaelite picture, rather vulgar.

7th April 1953, *Tuesday*

Beautiful cool night after the rain and a lovely fresh morning all dewy and sparkling. The driver of the watercart sitting on the bar of his cart. Horns of the cattle like lyres forming a beautiful motive.

To Mysore with N and Srinivasin before lunch. Do some extensive shopping of paints, etc.

Back to find the third colour of Dua's poster well printed. More thunder and rain with yet another spectacular sunset and a clear view of the distant hills. This I gather will now be a daily feature till the monsoon breaks in June.

8th April 1953, *Wednesday*

A prolonged thunderstorm during the night with heavy rain. Country fresh this morning and seems already

Towards dusk a first burst of
rain. Wonderful Stormy Sunset.
Great Rainbow. Flashes of
lightning.

Sunday 5th — Kharagpur : early morning.
Breakfast at the Multiple. Service by 9.00.
Das's 2nd Column goes on well — Visit
by Eagleton accompanied by Badrial & others.

Temperature much cooler owing to rain in
the neighbourhood, though no rain here.
Cloudy sky which makes country look very much
like England. A productive day.
Air India tell me that they can book
my flight for the 30th.

greener, though this probably imagination. A bit cold and funked bathing at the well. Second silk screen poster finished. Not too good, should have supervised more. Walked into Yalwal after lunch to see the trainees decorating walls. Designs, alas, a little banal. Should have had gods and goddesses — more decorative.

The usual thundery weather — sky lit with sheet lightning all round the horizon.

9th April 1953, *Thursday*

Into Mysore with N and Srinivasin after lunch. Some hurried shopping and look at the Teachers' Training College, our proposed next home. Found it wouldn't do for a variety of reasons. Chiefly that of wind, as no glazing to windows. Decide on Exhibition Buildings. Pick up Miss Rutherford, our new trainee. A quick cup of tea with Badriah and Eagleton. Dash back. Mix glue, size and colours and visit village. Trainees hard at work stencilling walls.

The vulgarity of some of the wall paintings made me squirm. Fear I showed it, which has caused some upset among the artists. In fact I hated the whole business, putting up our cheap little modern messes in a pretty village. The stencils, however, owing to the character quality and craft quality, have something to be said for them and not so offensive. If I had been a village elder I would have said the hell with the lot of us — interfering foreigners. The chrome lithos of gods and goddesses framed in the huts do the job better. Still, something in the stencil idea. Fear I will never be a social worker.

10th April 1953, *Friday*

Last day at the bungalow. Packing in the morning. An

afternoon trying to make a stencil design for cow and calf. Looks almost as vulgar as my trainees' work.

11th April 1953, *Saturday*

We move into Mysore. Sad saying goodbye to Yelwal Bungalow. Busy morning settling in to the Exhibition Buildings. N and I get rooms in the Chowmanish Bhavan[?]. Saiyid Din visits us with Badriah and others at the Exhibition Buildings in the afternoon. Hard work shifting goods. Tremendous thunderstorm at about 9.00 which lasted most of the night, with vivid lightning, a high wind and much rain. Town lights go out so to bed in the dark. Extremely hard bed, much noise so little sleep.

12th April 1953, *Sunday*

Morning at the Exhibition Buildings moving in. Visit again by Saiyid Din. Lunch at the India Bhavan. Fruitless wait for the carpenter in the afternoon. Slept well, though well bitten by the mosquitoes.

13th April 1953, *Monday*

A long day at the Exhibition Buildings and tired at the end of it. Can't draw in consequence.

14th April 1953, *Tuesday*

Lunch at the Carlton Hotel run by Catholic Indians (Parsees) in supposedly European style and inhabited by young Indian masters from St Philomena's College. The result like an Italian small country inn or hotel (a bad one), but beautiful to the eye and nostalgic of Europe. Lunch, omelettes and bad coffee. Use knives, spoons and forks. Take a party to the Wesley Press and conduct a pre-arranged questionnaire to the printer re new primer. Afternoon all to a village where we stencil walls, with horrible results. Later, council give film show in village street of films we had seen before. The village a very beautiful and clean one. N and I get back very late, excessively tired and dispirited after the stencil flop. How I hate making a mess of those beautiful white walls.

15th April 1953, *Wednesday*

A productive day at the Seminar. Abyan Khan's poster nearly finished. Dinner with Hussain and Bose at their home. Meat meal which tasted delicious. Tremendous storm of rain during night. Sorry for the poor musicians in the shack outside.

16th April 1953, *Thursday*

Abyan Khan's poster finished, a really professional-looking job. My drawings stuck up in morning. Two women from the shack in to clean it. To tea with Badriah. N, Eagleton, two Americans, and a Mr and Mrs Hart and some Indians there.

17th April 1953, *Friday*

Buy silk and organdie for the screen. In afternoon whole Seminar visits a food research establishment. Go round some rather spectacular looking laboratories full of strange apparatus but visit on the whole a bore.

18th April 1953, *Saturday*

With rest of Seminar by bus to visit a *Vidya pith*[12] about sixteen miles outside the town. Pass through pretty country, now very green with the recent rains. Many bullock carts, peasants, herds of goats, sheep and cattle on the road. The VP of no great interest. Stop at the neighbouring town to see the big temple. Everything massively carved and I thought a little boring . The

Elephant god, dancing figures (the best) and many erotic scenes carved in deep relief. These often charming, though quite shocking. Rain on the way home. The country looking even better under a grey sky and with many shining puddles. Many orchards of mango trees, with red ploughed earth between the tracks. Here and there palm gardens, dykes, paddy fields, a great tank or lake full of shining water. Blue range of the Nilghiri Mountains in the distance.

19th April 1953, *Sunday*

An outing with our trainees. Itinerary — a temple at the meeting of two rivers, Somnathpur and Srirangapatam. Country very beautiful and rich looking. Much water in the way of tanks and ditches. Earth red, land flat with alluvial soil. The green of young rice. Banana plantations, sugar cane. The roads (minor ones) lined by fine banyan trees and populous with flocks of goats, buffaloes, oxen, ox-drawn carts and sheep. Red mud villages with red tiled roofs and always distant views of blue hills. The temple at the junction of the rivers (mighty floods in monsoon time) now wide, shallow and sandy, standing on a pretty spit of land with shady trees and steps down to the water. Visited what looked like a small enclosed cemetery full of gravestones. They turned out to be votive stones put there by people wanting children. They were all carved with the snake emblem. Shown round by a weird-looking cleric, naked to the waist and carrying a little hand bowl. Hesitated to tip him as felt he might be the dean of the establishment. Didn't do so, as he did not seem to expect it. A number of other priests about. Paths clean and swept, trees sur-

like a small enclosed Cemetery full of they turned out to be volcanic stone put there by people + washing children

grave stones

rounded with flag-stones. A dead cobra on the ground and, but for the latter, much the feeling of a cathedral close.

Next to Somnathpur. A very old and now disused temple magnificently carved. Plan the same as others, rectangular enclosure lined with cell-like shrines for minor deities. The central block with tower richly carved all over. Gods, dancing figures, processions of elephants, horses and scenes from the *Ramayana*. Inside very dark and confined. Guide carried candle on a stick which gave little or no light. Our photographers very busy and I as usual am photographed from many angles together with the scenery. Most of the carving defaced by the Muslims. The general effect strange and rich but does not give me much pleasure. The detail only. From here to Srirangapatam. Halt on the way at a village coffee house full of nesting sparrows. First to Tipu Sultan's tomb which I found uninteresting but was tired by then. Found the small cemetery, full of graves of British soldiers and a few wives who had died in the first campaign, more affecting. Then to the summer palace and had a second look at the magnificent frescoes. N very busy taking colour photos of them. A great bough from one of Tipu's mango trees fell on a public bench below, while we were there. Luckily nobody sitting on the bench or they would have been killed.

Visited the fort but of no particular interest (visually). Back very late.

20th April 1953, Monday

Not a very productive day. First colour Haq's poster. Proof copy of *Tim in Danger* arrives.

Monday 20. — Not a very productive day. 1st slow. Hay's post. — Proof copy & Tim & Danya arrived.

Tuesday 21st. — Long day of ill humour. — Two small pieces of Hay's 2nd column. — quite & achievement. — Back late & very tired. Trekked to bed seven hours & turn.

21st April 1953, Tuesday

Long day at the Seminar. Two good prints of Haq's second colour. Quite an achievement. Back late and very tired. Treat the silk screen boys to rum.

22nd April 1953, Wednesday

A fruitless day. N in bed with a temperature. Haq makes the paint too thin, spoils a dozen prints and ends printing for the day. To Wesley Press in afternoon. Find Badriah has not clinched contract so held up there. To dinner in evening at the Mission Hospital. Matron, Miss R, a Wesleyan minister and wife, and young man in white. Hugh Warren from the Wesley Press and myself. A grand dinner but not much in the way of talk.

23rd April 1953, Thursday

Norman better but still confined to room. Better day at the Seminar. Haq's third colour goes on successfully. Organise a great spring clean. Gopal and Kallan arrive from Delhi. Return to find N holding court. Badriah, Tirmani, Gowda, then four students.

24th April 1953, Friday

Poor Galviya's poster doesn't go too well. A botched job, I am afraid. There seems no end to silk screen problems.

25th April 1953, Saturday

Disastrous morning with the litho plates. Plates from Bombay covered unknown to us with some sort of preservative which should have been washed off before drawing on. Taken by Hugh Warren after lunch to bathe in a delightful spot some ten miles outside Mysore. A shady, ruined temple by a dammed up bit of the River Cauvery. Women washing their clothes and themselves by the temple steps. An old man fishing. Cattle wading across the lower reaches of the river. Rocks and sands to bask on.

Evening to see a coffee planter and taxidermist. American wife, pretty and nice. Plied us with large whiskies and sodas. Back to hotel before dinner. Find N entertaining a number of students.

26th April 1953, *Sunday*

High Mass at the Cathedral at 7.00. The Bishop saying it. Nave packed with the prettiest throng imaginable of native women in their best saris. As many men and boys, too. All so much holier than we are that it puts us to shame.

To Seminar in morning and help cut a stencil and prepare squeegee for tomorrow's printing. Severely bitten last night and find a bug in my bed this morning. Have all my bedding out in the sun today. Spend afternoon and evening writing letters.

27th April 1953, *Monday*

Very hot night but slept well. Long day at the Seminar.

28th April 1953, *Tuesday*

Afternoon with Miss R to Wesley Press to print her plates. I fear a dismal failure. Haq's poster printed and looks very well.

29th April 1953, *Wednesday*

Irritating day at Seminar trying to cut stencils. Dinner with Hugh Warren in his bachelor establishment. Ardent young Methodist and strong against the papists. Doesn't know I'm one and wonder what his reaction will be when he knows. Takes me by car to Chamundi Hill. Bright moonlight and a strong cool breeze,

1000 ft. up. See a great stone bull, fine rocks and feathery trees. The lights of the city far below.

30th April 1953, *Thursday*

Lumbago and the universal complaint which have plagued me all day. Goodbye lunch to Dr Rutherford at the station restaurant. Late afternoon N and I taken by Warren to see taxidermist's family. Wife third daughter of O'Flaherty, the film man. Back to hotel at 7.00, returned to taxidermists for dinner. Guests: tx. and wife, two brothers, elderly mama and a bishop's wife, Warren and myself. Great storm. Get drenched getting from car to porch — two yards. Sit through dinner in my host's shirt and my own damp trousers. Make a social gaffe when I say that N and I want to live like Indians. Fear I am regarded as a dangerous revolutionary. (Communist intelligentsia.) Fierce glares from the brothers. In fact a disastrous evening resulting in an acute attack of piles from sitting in wet pants. Get back to find my room flooded, a miserable night in much pain.

1st May 1953, *Friday*

Wretched day. Condition still very painful. Wire from *Punch* asking me to make a full-page drawing for them. Not sure whether I can. [see page 10]

2nd May 1953, *Saturday*

Feel foul. Sit in my room till 11.20. Car to bank and back again. At 4.00 go with Hussains to Art Gallery. Contents an extraordinary jumble of bad Victoriana with a few pretty things among. Rajput little pictures. See a young man's funeral on way home. Corpse exposed and carried in bamboo litter decorated with leaves. Old men are not mourned which seems sensible.

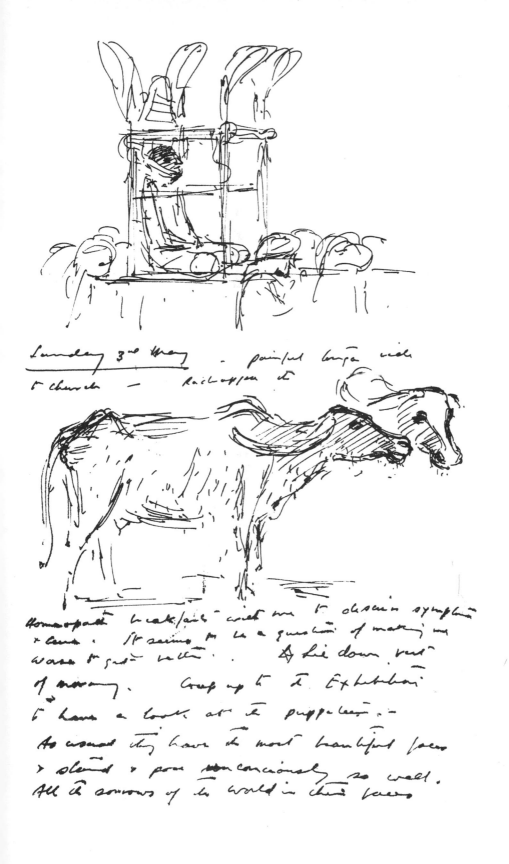

Sunday 3rd May — painful longer visit
to churches — Raichappen it

Homeopath breakfast with me to discuss symphonies
+ lunch. It seems to be a question of making me
warm to get well. A lie down rest
of morning. Creep up to the Exhibition
to have a look at the puppeteers. —
As usual they have the most beautiful faces
+ stand + pose unconsciously so well.
All the sorrows of the world in their faces

At 5.30 carried off to late tea with the Indian manager of the Mysore State Railway. Clever ambitious wife and two daughters in their teens, both very westernised. 7.00 p.m. puppet show at Exhibition Buildings. Shadow puppets. Fascinating flat transparent figures in bright colours. (Derain? illustrations to Rabelais.) Get home at 9.00, exhausted with continued pain.

3rd May 1953, *Sunday*

Painful tonga ride to church. Rajappan, the homeopath, breakfasts with me to discuss symptoms and cure. It seems to be a question of making me worse to get better. Lie down rest of morning. Go up to the Exhibition to have a look at the puppeteers. As usual they have the most beautiful faces and stand and pose unconsciously so well. All the sorrows of the world in their faces.

4th May 1953, *Monday*

Feel better after first good night's sleep for days. To nearby village with rest of Seminar. Decorate wall spaces with our stencils. My theory that they should be used in a strictly decorative manner I think justified. Monday is a holiday for the oxen and buffalo, so village full of resting cattle and idle carts. A very beautiful sight which, alas, I had no time to draw. Afternoon at Seminar stretching an organdie screen.

5th & 6th May 1953, *Tuesday & Wednesday*

N ill. Long days at Seminar, though not very arduous. Both nights out shopping in the town. Get *cholis*[13] made for C and Chris. Order a pair of trousers. The town, particularly the market, delightful at night. Cool with a thousand pleasant smells. The sharp smell of ripe mangoes, incenses, sandalwood and spices. Shops crowded, women buying saris. Must concentrate on drawings of shops and town life, particularly look for composition of figures. Shoppers leave their sandals on the step and squat barefoot on the floor. Only barbarians like myself wearing shoes into shops. Buy oranges, butter and marmalade for N in the market.

7th May 1953, *Thursday*

Finish Gurni's poster, thank God. Now only Kulkarni's left. How they bore me. Shopping in the evening. Nearly stumble on, in the dark, a small party of one woman and two children and a starving dog, all eating something unmentionable in the gutter. So very poor. The children like little dark spiders.

8th May 1953, *Friday*

Afternoon to children's book centre. Pathetic old chap. Idea that in some mysterious way we could in a word improve his publications. Bose organises a ceremony in honour of Tagore's[14] birthday. Gupte and Ganguli sing. Records. Srinivasin's daughter dances and Bose intones in a parsonical voice.

9th May 1953, *Saturday*

Seminar outing. I and trainees [take] third class train [to] Hassan. Bus to Sravanabelagola, climb steps to temple. Great statue. Back to Hassan. Dinner at *Vidya pith*. Concert afterwards. To bed on concrete floor at midnight.

10th May 1953, *Sunday*

Up at 5.00 to see round *Vidya pith*. Boiled wheat concoction for breakfast. Bus to Belur breaks down. The Temple. Bus now out of commission. Back Hassan by crowded public bus 2.00. No moment to myself in

Shoulder of rock exhausting & frightening.
Bilum much like other temples. Some fine
carvings of dancing girls. Don't like temples.
The train journey   some interiors of low
class coffee house.   most
rewarding pictorially.
So much to do
& no time.

The train
journey
from Hassan
back to Mysore
as interesting as
first. Carriage
crowded. Blind singer begging - The man
sleeping on the luggage rack

which to write or draw. In many ways a hideous two days — bad roads, break down omnibus, social obligations and extreme discomfort. The temple at Sravanabelagola fine when reached, but a climb of six hundred and fifty steps up a smooth face and very steep shoulder of rock exhausting and frightening. Belur much like other temples. Some fine carvings of dancing girls. *Don't like temples.* The train journey and some interiors of low-class coffee house most rewarding pictorially. So much to do and no time. The train journey from Hassan back to Mysore as interesting as first. Carriage crowded. Blind singers begging. The man sleeping in the luggage rack. Towards dusk the train ran through country which had just undergone a violent rain storm. Great puddles in the fields. Cataracts of water everywhere. A wonderful smell of wet earth. A lovely gleaming landscape in the half light. Return to find N no better. He has flu.

11*th May* 1953, *Monday*

Quiet day at Seminar. Nobody much inclined to work after our strenuous weekend. K's first colour goes wrong and has to be scrapped.

12*th May* 1953, *Tuesday*

An unhappy morning — K's poster won't work, find that white paint contains plaster of paris. Some major row brewing between Srinivasin senior and Marallapa and others. N still unwell. The afternoon goes from worse to worse. Very worried about N. Fear he has TB. So weak and temperature up at 4.00 every afternoon. Worried for him, also selfishly for myself. Afraid that I might have to wind up another Seminar — one even

more complicated than Delhi. In some ways I wish I
was not so horribly healthy. I am racked with pain but
frightfully fit. K's poster still going wrong. Have left
him and others too much to themselves. The result a
mess. Dinner Hugh Warren at Brindavan Gardens.

13th May 1953, *Wednesday*
Usual sort of day at Seminar. Work in room at night
writing letters.

14th May 1953, *Thursday*
N's X-ray shows that he has congestion of the lungs,
however on the mend. He is up but will have to go
slow. Better news than what I feared.

15th May 1953, *Friday*
Return to Exhibition Buildings to help with printing
and photographing Gupte poster. Left 1.00 a.m. Job in
a mess.

16th May 1953, *Saturday*
Sit in hotel room. Idle when I should have been writing
or drawing.

17th May 1953, *Sunday*
6.00 a.m. Mass. Morning spent working out design for
Exhibition folder. Afternoon with Norman concocting
reports. After dark, stroll to market. So beautiful —
goblin market. Great creamy white pumpkins, golden
gourds, pineapples, great bunches of bananas, mangoes
and wonderful vegetables. The smell of syringa from
the flower stalls, the sharp smell of mangoes, incense
from the incense shops. Would take months of constant
visiting to draw it. Moving but so frustrating in consequence. On way home meet procession of women in
brilliant saris, covered with gold. Their faces covered

and arms and legs jangling with bangles in some wedding procession. Streets at night always beautiful.

18th & 19th May 1953, Monday & Tuesday
Alas, mounting pressure of work. Exhibition Monday week. Reports to write, notes for cyclostyling, no time even to scribble. Undertaken to design and print a folder for the Exhibition. Use Selectarian method, two colours. Hope and pray we don't make a mess of it.

20th & 21st May 1953, Wednesday & Thursday
Great difficulties with our folders. Finish printing 2.30 on Thursday morning. Luckily Badriah seems pleased, though I fear they look pretty rough. To town hall to get cholera injection. Give a talk to local Rotarians on work of Seminar. What a bunch.

22nd, 23rd & 24th May 1953, Friday, Saturday & Sunday
Preparing Exhibition. Events — Friday trainees' tea party. Saturday party at Arniza's. Sunday Shukla arrives. Experts' dinner party to trainees. Exhibition begins to take shape. Exhausted.

25th May 1953, Monday
All goes according to plan. Show looks quite well. The usual interminable speeches to a large audience. My vote of thanks to the Minister and students. Stagger back to the hotel and drink a quarter bottle of rum before I recover.

26th May 1953, Tuesday
Busy with Shukla on winding up arrangements. Give a recorded talk over radio.

27th May 1953, Wednesday
Catch the night train to Bangalore. N and half the Seminar to see me off after a large gathering in my room at

the hotel with much rum drunk. Am garlanded with many garlands of clematis. Later these scent the whole carriage. A sad goodbye to so many friends.

28th May 1953, Thursday

Arrive Bangalore at 5.30 a.m. after an uneasy night in the train during which the rain dripped on me through the leaky windows. No Council van to meet me. Find the modern Hindu and Western Hotel full but get into the Central. Morning spent fixing insurance, income tax, etc. Afternoon sleeping and drawing the *Punch* job.

29th May 1953, Friday

Off at dawn by Deccan Airways to Bombay. Change at Hyderabad. A smooth flight. Put up at the Taj[15] — magnificent Victorian mausoleum. Alarms and much tiresome waiting in afternoon. Lloyds Bank very kind in getting me out of my difficulty re travellers' cheques, but it meant waiting in their offices for the best part of two anxious hours before problem solved.

30th May 1953, Saturday

Goodbye to India.

NOTES

NOTES

1. Mrs Doris Chaning Pearce, niece of Ardizzone's wife, Catherine (p.23)

2. Now the Yamuna River (p.23)

3. Humayun: (1508–56) Mogul emperor of Delhi, father of Akbar the Great (p.35)

4. William Chaning Pearce, MBE, KPM, an officer of the Indian Police, on special duty in Delhi at this time as Director of Enforcement to deal with the black market in cloth. He was one of the few British officers who stayed on to serve the new independent India, retiring in 1958 (p.36)

5. *The Forsyte Saga* by John Galsworthy; illustrated edition 1948 with drawings by Anthony Gross (p.39)

6. This appeared in the Coronation Issue, June 1953 (p.98)

7. Holi: one of the major Hindu festivals. The distinguishing feature of this spring festival is the throwing of coloured powders and liquids at people (p.109)

8. Nicky: Nicholas, the youngest of Edward and Catherine Ardizzone's children (p.115)

9. Probably the Brindavan Gardens at Krishnarajasagar (p.120)

10. *machan*: trap (p.123)

11. Tipu Sultan: (1749–99) Sultan of Mysore. His intrigues with the French to stir up war against the English eventually led to the storming of his capital, Srirangapatam, by the English during which Tipu himself was killed (p.126)

12. *Vidya pith:* a rural college where students on a six-month course are trained in rural handicrafts at proficiency level (p.134)

13. *Choli:* warm embroidered waistcoat. 'C and Chris' are Catherine and Christianna Ardizzone, E.A.'s wife and daughter (p.147)

14. Tagore, Sir Rabindranath (1861–1941): Indian poet and philosopher, Nobel Prize winner for literature 1913 (p.148)

15. Taj Mahal Hotel (p.155)